FRANCIS, *Bishop of Rome*

THE GOSPEL FOR THE THIRD MILLENNIUM

ALLAN FIGUEROA DECK, SJ

Paulist Press
New York / Mahwah, NJ

Front jacket images: Background photo of Patagonian Argentine route by leojerez / Bigstock.com; image of Pope Francis from photo by Filippo Monteforte / Associated Press, © 2015 The Associated Press
Jacket design by Lightly Salted Graphics
Book design by Lynn Else

Library of Congress Cataloging-in-Publication Data

Deck, Allan Figueroa, 1945–
    Francis, Bishop of Rome : the gospel for the third millennium / Allan Figueroa Deck, SJ.
        pages cm
    Includes bibliographical references.
    ISBN 978-0-8091-0622-6 (hardcover : alk. paper) — ISBN 978-1-58768-543-9 (ebook)
    1. Francis, Pope, 1936– 2. Popes—Biography. I. Title.
    BX1378.7.D43 2016
    282.092—dc23
    [B]

                                                                    2015016555

ISBN 978-0-8091-0622-6 (hardcover)
ISBN 978-1-58768-543-9 (e-book)

Published by Paulist Press
997 Macarthur Boulevard
Mahwah, New Jersey 07430

www.paulistpress.com

Printed and bound in the
United States of America

For my sister Armida Deck (1940–2015),
a resourceful woman of action who loved life,
her neighbor, and God with astonishing zest

CONTENTS

FOREWORD

People long to know the famous, those known and respected around the world. They like to feel close to celebrities, to have their pictures taken with them, to get their autograph. But most renown become known only superficially, on the surface without an in-depth grasp of the person and how they came to be who they are. The public rarely knows who were the teachers of these individuals, who formed their worldview.

Allan Deck delves deeply into the person of Francis, Bishop of Rome, well known and greatly loved around the world. Through research and personal interviews, Deck explores the pope's roots, gains insights about the man from those who knew Bergoglio in his early formation, and explores his immigrant roots and how Argentinian culture and Jesuit formation have affected him. Deck delves into the thoughts and writings of those who had an impact on Pope Francis, those who influenced how he thinks, writes, and acts. By exploring the tapestry of influences on the person of the Holy Father, Deck gives us a glimpse into the origins of his passion for the poor, his embrace of mercy, and his determination to lead a church of missionary disciples from maintenance to mission.

Everywhere I go, when I ask those with whom I am speaking what they think of Pope Francis, they say without hesitation, "We love him." Their faces light up and often they applaud for a long time. His entrance on the world stage truly has taken hold of the imagination of so many around the world. People want to know more about him. This book captures the person of Francis. It is far more than a biography, but the book lays out how he came to be the man he is and the pope he has become.

I was in the seminary at the same time Bergoglio entered formation as a Jesuit in 1958. Seminary around the world was rules-focused.

Obedience to the rule was paramount. The goal of seminary was to take you out of the world and its influences and immerse you in the spiritual life.

My formation at the University of St. Mary of the Lake in Mundelein, Illinois, although preparing me to be a diocesan priest in the Archdiocese of Chicago, was directed by Jesuits and was grounded in the Spiritual Exercises of Ignatius. We learned the Ignatian examen. We were taught how to pray with our imagination, to immerse ourselves in the Scriptures. But we were not taught "apostolic boldness," which has characterized the Jesuit apostolate and which Pope Francis has embraced. Remember how he called young people at World Youth Day to go back home and stir things up.

Deck sees Bergoglio's Ignatian formation as training him to "Fear not" and instead wholeheartedly embrace Vatican II, putting aside the caution that has gripped the Church after Vatican II. Pope Francis calls the Church to be bold and faithful. If all we are is bold, we will drift off from our moorings and be hopelessly lost. If all we are is faithful, we could become hopelessly irrelevant in the world.

Deck traces the influences of CELAM and its founders on Bergoglio's thought. This reached fullest expression at Aparacida where Bergoglio had a major hand in fashioning its final document. Medellín and Puebla powerfully influenced the Holy Father with the importance of popular religiosity, a notion Deck has explored in many of his previous writings. "Popular culture, including popular religion, constitutes the most important field for sowing the Word of God for evangelization" (see p. 38).

Deck explores at length the impact of two diocesan priests, Lucio Gera and Rafael Tello as well as Marcello Azevedo. It is fascinating to hear the distant echoes of their thinking in the thoughts and writings of Pope Francis. Everyone's thoughts and insights develop through what one experiences, reads, and studies. This book encourages those who want to know more about Francis's thoughts to delve into these theologians who have had some impact on his thinking. Clearly Pope Francis has had the works of these theologians on his book shelf, and I suspect they are well worn.

Pope Francis learned and has embraced a desire not to shun the modern world but to strive to engage the culture in dialogue.

Monsignor Daniel Cantwell was a priest of the Archdiocese of Chicago with whom I had the privilege to serve for several years and who had a profound influence on my thinking about Church. I heard him once say that he saw the Church as groping, not pontificating, moving, not standing still, a Church on the move. He did not see the Church as set over and against the world but as the breath of the world that liberates from pettiness, smallness, and despair. It revels in friendship, love, and eating together. Clearly Pope Francis is encouraging such engagement with modernity. We can learn from the world, and we have much to teach the world.

What I appreciate most about this book is the articulation of the emerging pastoral vision being presented to the Church by Pope Francis through the tried and true process of "see-judge-act"—a pastoral process long proposed in the CELAM documents. Deck focuses on the Holy Father's push to get the Church to "go out" and not "hunker down"; to take on a true pastoral imagination in carrying out its mission.

The emerging role of the laity and their responsibility, flowing from their baptism, to be missionary disciples is key to the realization of Francis's pastoral vision. We cannot be a Catholic Church without an ordained priesthood, but we will not realize the Church's mission until all the members of the baptized take their rightful place in carrying on the mission of Christ.

In 2005, the United States Conference of Catholic Bishops issued a document called "Co-Workers in the Vineyard" that held up the importance of the laity's engagement in the marketplace and in the Church. Both spheres need the involvement of the laity. Such involvement can be the leaven leading to the growth of the Church reminiscent of the phenomenal embrace of the gospel reported in the Acts of the Apostles.

Key among the many takeaways from the Holy Father's young papacy lifted up by Deck in his book is the focus on social justice, the engagement of the Church with the poor, the marginalized, the littlest and weakest among us. Francis's example has moved me to reflect on how I, as a bishop, can focus my ministry on social issues prevalent in my diocese like homelessness, poverty, addictions, mental illness, and the plight of immigrants and refugees. Francis strikingly calls the

Church a "field hospital" where people can find relief, healing, mercy, and comfort.

While I do not agree with every point Deck makes in this book or with every implication that could be drawn from those points, I believe there is much to be learned about the person of Francis and his pastoral vision from reading this well-researched volume.

Bishop Gerald Kicanas
Tucson, Arizona

ACKNOWLEDGMENTS

I am especially grateful to Father Alejandro Bertolini for providing me with an excellent list of associates of Jorge Mario Bergoglio in Buenos Aires and Córdoba. This group provided me with copious background information on Jorge Mario Bergoglio and access to several scholars. One of those contacts was Professor Emilce Cuda of the Catholic University of Argentina (UCA), whose advice and guidance in mapping out research on my subject proved indispensable. Emilce's warm hospitality and that of her family were outstanding. The theological faculty of the UCA provided a great deal of data and pertinent advice that helped focus my thoughts. It was my good fortune to participate in the May 6, 2014, Symposium on the pastoral vision of Pope Francis at the UCA, during which I was exposed to a rich gamut of insights from a collegial group of scholars and church leaders who know Pope Francis better than any other group. Indeed, they continue to consult and contribute to Pope Francis's ongoing work. Among these scholars and church leaders are Archbishop Victor Manuel Fernández, Father Carlos María Galli, and Professor Virginia R. Azcuy. In addition, the writings of Jesuit Father Juan Carlos Scannone, one of Bergoglio's early professors, have been an important source of insight for me regarding the human and intellectual sources of Pope Francis's vision and leadership, as have the writings of Fathers Omar Albado and Enrique Ciro Bianchi, which opened to me the remarkable Argentine version of Liberation Theology, *La Teología del Pueblo*, and its principle exponents, Fathers Lucio Gera and Rafael Tello. This theology leaves more than a few traces in the thoughts and actions of the 266th pope.

The members of the Jesuit community at the Colegio del Salvador in downtown Buenos Aires were wonderful hosts during my visit, and I learned a great deal in conversation with Jesuit Fathers

Ignacio Pérez del Viso, Ignacio García Mata, and Salvador Verón Cárdenas. At the Catholic University of Córdoba (UCC), I had the good fortune of interviewing Jesuit Fathers Alfonso Gómez, rector of the UCC; one of Jorge Mario Bergoglio's novices, Carlos Cruz; and Oscar Calvo, one of Bergoglio's Jesuit contemporaries. Thanks to them and the community in Córdoba, my stay there was enlightening and enjoyable. At the Theological Faculty of the Jesuits in San Miguel, I was fortunate to meet and converse with Father Rafael Velasco.

The meeting with the association of alumni of the Jesuit secondary schools, especially with Mr. Roberto Poggio, one of several former students of Bergoglio with whom I shared a delicious meal at their annual gathering, was a valuable and thoroughly enjoyable experience. Their enthusiasm for the subject of my writing was infectious. Mr. Sergio Gabriel Raczko of the Video Studio at the Colegio del Salvador was an important dialogue partner for me as I pondered the direction that this book would take.

In both the journey to Argentina and later during the months of work on the manuscript, I was fortunate to count on the companionship, encouragement, and great sense of humor of Jesuit Father Michael J. Mandala. My Jesuit community at Loyola Marymount University and colleagues in the Department of Theological Studies were a constant source of support during this project as were my graduate assistants, Magalí del Bueno and Cristina Castillo. Cynthia Boland, administrative assistant for the Loyola Marymount University Jesuit community, provided much appreciated secretarial skills. My sister, Armida Deck, and lifelong friend, Teresita Basso, encouraged me at every turn during the months of research and writing. To them and to everyone mentioned here, I am deeply indebted.

For more than forty years, I have enjoyed the friendship of Father Virgilio Elizondo, who has been a wonderful mentor and inspiration for me and for two generations of Latino leaders in the United States. Father Virgilio suggested the title of this book and encouraged me all along the way in its production.

Finally, I am most grateful to Jesuit Father Thomas P. Rausch, my colleague at Loyola Marymount University, for recommending this project to Paul McMahon of Paulist Press. I appreciate Paul's patience and care in editing and moving this project to completion.

INTRODUCTION

The papacy of Argentine Jesuit Jorge Mario Bergoglio has been nothing less than spectacular. In a remarkably short time, his words, gestures, and executive actions have set in motion a transformation of both the papacy itself as well as the worldwide Roman Catholic Church. His arrival on the world scene has brought about a cottage industry in biographies and translations of his lively and relatively brief homilies and discourses. Monographic studies of Papa Bergoglio's stimulating thoughts are regularly reaching libraries and bookstores, while social media commentary grows by leaps and bounds. And, of course, the internet is abuzz. Pope Francis's penchant for off-the-cuff remarks, his straight-shooting commentary, and diligent reform of the Roman Curia and Vatican finances have all but annihilated the pervading mood of fear and malaise that led to his predecessor Pope Benedict XVI's resignation and to the College of Cardinals' decision to elect a steely man-of-action and relative outsider to clean up the mess. The first years of this pope's ministry have been absolutely momentous—even a bit frenetic—and he gives evidence of maintaining, if not accelerating, the pace of what some analysts have called his radical reforms.

There is little doubt that Pope Francis has won the heart of a world that finds itself in more than normal turmoil. Perpetual war in the Islamic world and beyond in the form of terrorism, mounting economic inequality, ecological degradation, shifting international roles and alliances, and all manner of vexing challenges to life and prosperity assault our minds and hearts day after day. On the global stage, Pope Francis appears as an always refreshing and often surprising source of wisdom, hope, and good humor in an otherwise bleak situation. At the time of his election, people who knew him well—like his sister María Elena—said that the new pope had become a "different man." At seventy-seven years of age, ready for retirement after fifteen years as leader of one of the largest and most diverse archdioceses in the world, Jorge Mario Bergoglio went to the 2013 conclave rather tired and ready for retirement. He had already arranged to live at a residence with some other retired priests and was thinking about how to maneuver the sometimes Byzantine process for naming new bishops in such a way as to get a good successor. Bergoglio bought a two-way ticket to the conclave and went to Rome thinking that this was going to be his Roman swan song.

Something happened, however, and Bergoglio, who had been a close contender in the 2005 conclave, quickly emerged as a favorite. The rest is history. Still, what lingers in one's thoughts in trying to put the pieces of this drama together are the mysterious and unexpected events that followed day after day from the very moment in which the new pope's tenure as Bishop of Rome and Vicar of Christ began. The list is mindboggling. First, there was the unprecedented name of Francis, then the totally unexpected Jesuit connection, and then the "New World Pope." But there was so much more. First, the extraordinary introduction of the new successor to Peter on the balcony of St. Peter's Basilica in which he changed the focus away from himself to the people of God in history, to the faithful assembled below in the piazza. He asked for their blessing first before giving them his own; second, he clearly signaled that some of the old protocols and tendencies toward ostentation in papal ceremonies were going to be revised; third, he returned to his hotel the next day to pay the bill himself; and fourth, he decided to separate himself from the control of the prevailing and questionable system he was being called to reform by choosing to live in Domus Santae Marthae rather than the Papal Palace. These gestures augured even more serious changes down the line, and with considerable dispatch, the new pope established a now familiar, take-charge pattern characterized by humility, candor, and plenty of humor.

More than two years into this papacy, is it now possible to see where matters are going and explore in some detail the sources of the "radical reform" unfolding before our very eyes? These questions fascinated me because of my lifelong involvement with the two main sources of Pope Francis's inspiration, namely, Latin American Catholicism and the Jesuits. I read everything I could get my hands on, especially in Spanish, the language in which virtually all the sources affecting Bergoglio have been written. In May of 2014, I traveled to Argentina to get to know some of the places and people that have been part of this extraordinary man's life. There I had the good fortune of meeting a group of outstanding academics at the Catholic University of Argentina who opened their homes, their lives, and their scholarship to me. I also met many Jesuits who knew Jorge Mario quite well—both those who identified with him and those who for various reasons have had personal difficulties with him. They all agreed that, while one may argue about his tenure as provincial superior of the Jesuits, his tenure as bishop and archbishop had been nothing less than outstanding.

Those weeks in Argentina allowed me to see the font where he was baptized, the confessional where he first sensed God's call to be a priest, the places where he lived as a young boy, where he attended Mass, and went to school. I visited and celebrated Mass in his cathedral on the Plaza de Mayo. In the sprawling Jesuit compound in San Miguel on the outskirts of Buenos Aires, I visited Bergoglio's room when he was superior of this community, and I even took a siesta on his bed! In this simple, austere bedroom, I noticed a statue of St. Joseph in a pose I had never before seen. It was Joseph, the husband of Mary, lying down, asleep and dreaming. Apparently, this portrayal of Joseph is not uncommon in Argentina. It struck me as particularly fitting for understanding this pope. Like Joseph, he is a guardian of Jesus and of the fledgling Church of which Mary is a model. The Holy Spirit—the source of Mary's fecundity in giving birth to Jesus—communicates in mysterious ways and is inspiring Bergoglio just as he inspired Joseph.

I returned convinced that what is happening in the Church is something rooted in its New Testament origins, a true reform that goes back to the most authentic sources. It is an astonishing time of grace. What Pope Francis is doing is perhaps comparable in impact to the Gregorian Reform of the eleventh century or even the Catholic Reformation in terms of its real consequences for the papal institution and down the line for world Catholicism. Pope Francis is wrestling with nothing less than "epochal change," the very term that he borrows from the landmark 2007 Document of Aparecida of the Latin American Bishops and uses in *Evangelii gaudium*.[1]

Papa Bergoglio means business and, as many Catholics have intuitively observed, the Holy Spirit is behind this surprising spring-time, the stunning renewal of and recommitment to the spirit of the Second Vatican Council. That Council first proposed the urgent need of reform and renewal in order to engage the modern world with openness and joy rather than hunker down in fear and irrelevance. For various reasons, the remarkable papacies of John Paul II and Pope Benedict XVI and their many accomplishments, had given "mixed signals" and engaged in an interpretation of the Second Vatican Council that gave too much credit to fear and allowed a deadening traditionalism to keep the Church back from fully carrying out its evangelizing mission.[2] The key to Pope Francis's stunning orientation to renewal and radicalness is found in the phrase "freshness of the Gospel." This book is a modest, first effort to look a bit more deeply into the sources and possible direction of his strong pastoral orienta-tion and surprising openness.

The profound Latin American experience of this pope, espe-cially his highly successful participation in the pastoral reflection, planning, and writing projects of CELAM, the Latin American Conference of Bishops, is a fundamental source of inspiration and guidance for him as was his role as president of the committee entrusted with producing the *Concluding Document of Aparecida*.[3] To assist in keeping on track with powerful pastoral tools and a clear-sighted vision, Pope Francis enjoys the friendship and support of an outstanding group of theologians and pastoralists. Among them are Archbishop Victor Manuel Fernández, Carlos Maria Galli, Virginia Azcuy, and Diego Fares.

A second source of inspiration that can be viewed as highly syn-ergistic with the Latin American pastoral-theological vision of this pope is his Jesuit and Ignatian formation. Francis is an extremely accomplished expert on the Society of Jesus and especially on the *Spiritual Exercises* of St. Ignatius. In innumerable ways, this heritage helps explain who this man is, the source of his seemingly boundless energy, and where he seeks to lead the Church.

This book is a wide-ranging effort to look at the direction of Pope Francis's papacy from the vantage point of his Latin American and Jesuit heritage. What does this tell us about the nature and deeper meaning of the reform he is leading, and where might it be going in terms of several areas of Church life, particularly its engagement with people pastorally and in its social teachings?

Chapter 1 recapitulates Pope Francis's fairly well-known biography with an effort to flag some of the key circumstances and moments in that life that correlate with his Petrine ministry today. Chapter 2 explores the Jesuit and Ignatian roots of this pope, who has steeped himself in the Jesuit ethos over a lifetime. Some indications are given about how that ethos has worked its way into many features of his way of proceeding, particularly his emphasis on an encounter with a merciful God in the person of Jesus Christ and his extraordinary freedom, a fundamental condition for both personal and collective discernment in the Church. Chapter 3 provides a more detailed overview of the enthusiastic and distinctive Latin American response to the Second Vatican Council's invitation to reform and renewal. Pastoral developments like the base ecclesial communities, breakthroughs in Catholic social teaching, and considerable controversy around Liberation Theology marked this creative period of more than half a century that spanned the years of priestly and episcopal ministries of Jorge Mario Bergoglio. Chapter 4 explores the thought of a particularly respected Argentine theologian, Rafael Tello, for whom Cardinal Bergoglio has expressed great admiration. Tello's conception of the Church as the faithful people of God in history and of the role of popular culture in the process of the inculturation of faith are notions deeply cherished by Pope Francis. The fifth chapter analyzes the pastoral orientation of this pope based on his familiarity with pastoral visioning and planning characteristic of Latin American Catholicism for the past fifty years. This chapter shows how the pastoral orientation dovetails with the Ignatian emphasis on spirituality and discernment. Chapter 6 highlights the central role played by the Church's understanding of its evangelizing mission in Pope Francis's reform agenda. Building on the emphasis his predecessors have given to the missionary character of the entire Church, this chapter explores the manifold ways in which this vision defines the pope's ministry today, its implications on practical matters of ecclesiology and the configuration of ministry. Chapter 7 expands on the significance of what is called pastoral-missionary conversion in the *Concluding Document of Aparecida* and in Pope Francis's "magna carta," *Evangelii gaudium*. The implications of this development are especially relevant to specific areas of the Church's life such as priestly formation, models of the parish, the role of the sacraments, and sociopolitical participation. The conclusion attempts to draw some specific implications in terms of key issues. What emerges is the beginning of a picture of where the Church in the United States of America may actually be going in the revolutionary age of Pope Francis.

This work is written for a general audience with some knowledge of Catholicism. It is meant to be a popular work rather than a scholarly one. The purpose is to take the analysis of Francis's tenure as pope to a deeper level of insight by correlating some of the events, people, circumstances, and experiences in his long life to his energetic activities and unfolding vision for the Church moving forward. How might his particular antecedents—Latin American, Argentine, and Jesuit—nourish his remarkable first years in office and illuminate the deeper practical significance and implications of what he brings to the Church for the faithful people of God in history?

Chapter One

SETTING THE STAGE

Spanish theologian Xavier Pikaza has referred to Argentina and specifically Buenos Aires as a fundamental *locus theologicus* for our times. He is referring to a concept of an earlier Spanish theologian, the sixteenth-century Dominican Melchor Cano, who conceived of *locus theologicus* as referring to sources for theological reflection such as the Sacred Scriptures themselves, the Church's traditions, the lives of great saints, and so forth. In singling out Argentina as a source for theological reflection today, Pikaza points to the profound impact that Buenos Aires roots have had on the life, ministry, and vision of the 266th pope.[1] Not only is Bergoglio the first Latin American and Jesuit pope, he is also the first ordained after the Second Vatican Council and the first to be the product of an immense, diverse, urban cultural zone not quite like any other in Latin America. When one investigates the background and inspiration for his refreshing pastoral concerns and approaches, one discovers a cadre of Argentine theologians and pastoralists centered primarily at the Universidad Católica Argentina (UCA) and the Faculty of Philosophy and Theology of the Jesuits in San Miguel, a suburb of Buenos Aires. This chapter seeks to introduce readers unfamiliar with this world to that rich environment of family, friends, teachers, local culture, and the faithful who have influenced Jorge Mario Bergoglio's thoughts and actions. This provides a context for later connecting the dots between his unique social, religious, political, and cultural environment on the one hand, with his startling, even revolutionary, way of proceeding as pope on the other. In a relatively brief time, Pope Francis has set in motion serious reforms and fostered new attitudes that go to the very heart of Catholicism today. How does his unique background help explain these unexpected and happy developments?

IMMIGRANT ROOTS

Jorge Bergoglio's story is first and foremost part of the persistent, worldwide reality of migration. Among the firsts one may ascribe to this Argentine pope, beyond the ones already mentioned, are his pronounced immigrant roots. Throughout history, people have been on the move, but certainly the nineteenth and the twentieth centuries were times of intense movement, especially for Southern Europeans—among them, of course, Italians like the Bergoglios and the Sívoris of Jorge's paternal and maternal sides, respectively. The father, Mario José, migrated to Argentina from Portacomaro in the province of Asti in Piedmont. He found a soul mate in Regina María, a first generation Argentine, whose mother was an immigrant with origins in Genoa, and whose father was a carpenter and native of Piedmont like the Bergoglios.

Initially, the Bergoglios did quite well financially in their adopted country. They came to Argentina in the early decades of the twentieth century, an extraordinary time of prosperity. Jorge's grandfather, Giovanni Angelo, decided to join his brothers, who had moved to South America after World War I to establish an exciting new business in Paraná, the capital of Entre Ríos province and a thriving boomtown. They produced asphalt for new highways and roads being built at a time of unprecedented growth. Mario José arrived in 1930 along with the rest of Giovanni Angelo's family just in time to experience the depression of the 1930s, which soon required the family to move to the working class barrio of Flores in Buenos Aires, where they opened a small dry goods store. Mario José had already earned his degree as an accountant in Italy and consequently found work as a bookkeeper in a stocking factory across the street from the Bergoglio residence.[2]

EARLY *PORTEÑO* INFLUENCES[3]

Thus began the process by which Jorge's family put down roots in the Flores district, one of the larger and more prominent of the many sections that make up Greater Buenos Aires. Jorge was the first of five children born to Mario José and Regina. Interestingly, they had met at a Salesian oratory and, in 1935, were married on

December 12, the feast of Our Lady of Guadalupe. Their first son, Jorge, was born almost exactly a year later and baptized in the magnificent Salesian shrine called María Auxiliadora, also in the Flores section. The Salesians have been extremely influential in Latin America and especially in Argentina given their strong Italian origins. Their charism stresses care for poor youth and young adults as well as the promotion of Catholic social teaching. Our Lady of Guadalupe was originally a Mexican devotion to Mary, one that, over five centuries, has become the signature Marian devotion of Latin America and more recently the United States. Many decades later, in the practice and writings of Jorge Bergoglio, the themes of concern for the poor (especially youth), Catholic social teaching (especially the inadequacies of "savage capitalism"), and the centrality of the Virgin Mary's witness for the Church's evangelizing mission constitute powerful, recurring motifs in all his ministries as a Jesuit, bishop, archbishop, and now as pope.[4]

Jorge was fortunate to have his paternal grandparents living close by. From them, he learned to speak their Piedmontese dialect of Italian. More important, Jorge had ongoing contact with his grandmother, Rosa, who, as he has noted frequently, was the single most important influence on his religious and spiritual life. Consequently, Jorge Bergoglio manifested a dominant trait of Catholicism of Latin America, an aspect of his religious and spiritual formation that was to become a decisive influence on his attitudes and ideas regarding what it means to evangelize. The fact that women and especially mothers and grandmothers are frequently heralded as the principle evangelizers or teachers of the faith in Latin America is a datum that helps trace the particular vision of the new evangelization spelled out in the 2007 *Concluding Document of Aparecida* and in Pope Francis's most definitive communication to date, *Evangelii gaudium*.

This background may also be a source of inspiration for Pope Francis's repeated calls for a deeper theology of women in the Church and for their more incisive participation in the Church's life. In his first greeting at the Angelus on March 17, 2013, to illustrate his kerygmatic theme of God's unconditional love and mercy, Pope Francis gave the example of a pious lady who wanted to go to confession and grasped quite well the central truth of God's mercy. Father Bergoglio jokingly asked the lady whether she had any sins and, if she did, whether God really would forgive them. She answered without hesitation that of course God would forgive them because he always does. Impressed by the lady's theological acumen, Bergoglio playfully replied, "Madam, did you study at the Gregorian?"[5] Moreover, in his first conversation with the International Theological Commission, Pope Francis raised the subject of the *sensus fidelium* and how it might be properly understood.[6] The term *sensus fidelium* refers to a faithful intuition of the baptized given by the Holy Spirit whereby the faith of the Church is preserved from error. Having experienced and benefitted so much in his own life from the simple but Spirit-filled faith of laywomen like Grandmother Rosa, Francis likes to raise this awareness and remind his listeners that fidelity to the gospel is advanced by the whole Church as the people of God and not just by its male hierarchical leaders or predominantly male academic theologians.

LOWER MIDDLE-CLASS ORIGINS

By all reports, Jorge enjoyed a fulfilling and happy youth even though the family was not very well off. Vacations, for example, were not possible given the family's tight budget, but certainly nothing was lacking, especially good food and access to education and health care. Jorge went to public schools, which in Argentina at the time, probably had the feel of Catholic schools, because the population was so overwhelmingly Catholic and religion was even offered as part of the curriculum. But he also experienced the anticlericalism typical of Latin American intellectuals who, since the nineteenth century, had been formed by teachers influenced by, if not imbued with, the spirit of the Enlightenment and French Jacobinism. Nevertheless, Jorge was exposed to a rich humanistic and scientific formation where he excelled in literature and was to earn a degree in chemistry.

The origins of his flair for literature, music, and excellent speaking and writing in a clear, lucid Spanish have much to do with the culturally rich environment of his Italo-Argentine home. In his eleven years of priestly formation as a Jesuit, he was further formed in Spanish as well as Latin, German, and Western literatures; philosophy; theology; and the humanities. Of course, this humanistic orientation includes what today is called high culture but also popular culture. Jorge Bergoglio, for instance, is quick to share with others his love of cooking, of soccer, and yes, of listening and dancing to the lurid strains of the archetypical *Porteño* music and dance called *tango* and to its even more popular expression called *milonga*.[7] Even more notable is the fact that already by the 1940s, when Jorge was growing up, Buenos Aires had become one of the more diverse cities of Latin America with its huge cohorts of immigrants, a uniquely cosmopolitan magnate that attracted people from all over the world. The immigrants were not only from Southern Europe but also from Eastern Europe—Armenians, Ukranians, Lebanese, and of course, Eastern European Jews. After New York, Buenos Aires has the largest population of Jews in the Americas. One cannot help but realize that the seeds of Jorge Bergoglio's fascination with what later he was to call the "culture of encounter" were first sown in the fertile soil of the great cosmopolitan center of Buenos Aires that was to be home for most of his life.

POLITICS: "ONE OF THE HIGHEST FORMS OF CHARITY"

Buenos Aires was also the center of tremendous political ferment. It is generally ignored today, but the first half of the twentieth century was an extraordinary time of boom and bust for Argentina, which went from being economically on the first tier of nations to a dramatically lower place—all within the first decades of the twentieth century.[8] Jorge Bergoglio was born into this Argentine world of boom and bust. The struggle of the poor and disenfranchised was something Jorge became aware of early in life along with the lack of solidarity among the social classes. This constituted for him a matter of grave concern to which he was to return often in his writing and preaching as archbishop. Being a child of the lower middle class, raised in a quintessentially lower middle class barrio, and a product of public schools rather than the more prestigious and exclusive Catholic schools undoubtedly left on him a sharp sense of social justice and more than a tinge of egalitarianism. Decades later as archbishop and pope, he would like to quote Pope Pius XI, who said, "Politics is one of the highest forms of charity."[9] While insisting that the Church itself is to avoid partisan politics and ideological polarizations, Bergoglio has a keen interest in politics understood as concern for matters of public policy, especially when it deals with the poor and excluded. Those who know Pope Francis very well contend that he is a great manager and administrator, an excellent strategist, and a consummate *político* in the sense of practicing the art of the possible.[10] The astonishing way in which he is producing substantive changes in Vatican financial affairs, the Procrustean Roman Curia, and the Catholic Church's worldwide image is proof of this pope's extraordinary ability to produce real outcomes. And he has just begun!

The political struggles that have attended the series of dramatic socioeconomic declines of Argentina in Jorge Bergoglio's lifetime were severe and emotionally charged. They continue to be so to the present day. Consequently, it is no wonder that a perceptive and supremely energetic person like Jorge Bergoglio took a deep interest in politics from an early age. He read up on the various political movements of the time like fascism, which was on the rise precisely in the nations of origin of most Argentines—Italy, Spain, and Germany. Bergoglio's first serious reading in political theory was actually on communism. The supervisor of his high school job at a chemical laboratory exposed him to international communism and socialism, which in the twentieth century, had great appeal in Latin America, especially to intellectuals and workers, where the oppressive history of European colonialism and liberalism, that is, *laisse faire* capitalism and economic dependency, had left the popular masses with a decidedly bitter taste and a corresponding drive to find alternatives.

In this regard, Bergoglio likes to tell the story of the impact made on him by Esther Ballestrino de Careaga, a died-in-the-wool Paraguayan communist and his supervisor at the laboratory where he worked. She gave him the first books he ever read on political theory.[11] Of course, he never bought in to these theories, but he learned early in life that political opponents, people who think differently from oneself about politics and policy, can be very good people and may also be right in at least some respects. Years later, when right-wing commentator Rush Limbaugh charged Pope Francis with dabbling in pure Marxism, the pope replied, "Marxist ideology is wrong. But I have met many Marxists in my life who are good people, so I don't feel offended."[12] Of course, for Bergoglio, it was not only from people of a left-wing persuasion like Esther that he ostensibly gained a critical view of the socioeconomic and political reality of Argentina and the rest of Latin America. Catholic social teaching as disseminated by his many Salesian contacts and their emphasis on social justice were perhaps even more influential sources of inspiration for this thoughtful, committed young man. The Salesians were main actors on the ecclesial scene in mid-twentieth-century Buenos Aires, and they introduced Bergoglio to the major themes and principles of the great social encyclicals: *Rerum novarum* and *Quadragesimo anno*. Bergoglio's early life corresponded to the period in which Catholic Action and Young Christian Workers flourished in the Catholic countries of Europe and throughout Latin America. These movements also took much of their inspiration from Catholic social teaching just as the Catholic labor movement of the first half of the twentieth century did in the United States. In addition, out of these experiences, Liberation Theology and its distinctive Argentine version called *La Teología del Pueblo* would eventually emerge.

PERONISM

It was Bergoglio's destiny to live through the heady years of the meteoric rise of the *caudillo*, Juan Domingo Perón, and of his charismatic first wife, Evita Duarte. In 1946, when Jorge was ten years old, Perón came into power and laid the foundations for what was to become the defining political framework for Argentine politics ever since, namely, the elusive but potent ideology of Peronism. Some have even charged Bergoglio with being a Peronist—a Buenos Aires journal declared, "The Vatican: New Scene of Peronist Intrigue."[13] Over decades, Peronism has come to be identified by many with manipulation of the popular masses and with inconsistent and unprincipled opportunism. Whatever be the subsequent track record of Perón's followers, the fact, however, is that Juan Domingo Perón's first term as president was a remarkable period of social advancement for the Argentine working class. For example, the average wage of workers increased by one third in Perón's first five years. The number of unionized workers became the highest in Latin America, and significant progress was made in access to medical care, social security, and education for ordinary Argentines.[14] These accomplishments together with the charitable concerns of Evita, seem to have etched Peronism in the very DNA of the Argentine popular classes, both urban and rural.

While there is an enormous ambiguity about the real accomplishments of Perón and Evita, as well as those of their political heirs (whose political leanings go from extreme progressivism to extreme conservatism), one might argue that Bergoglio, either by osmosis or purposefully, has picked up important traits of Peronism that serve him very well: first, Peronism's drive toward inclusion of and concern for all social classes and the most forgotten elements of society; second, the ability to successfully communicate with the broadest possible audience; third, an ability to avoid or transcend narrow ideologies of left and right; and fourth, a resulting popularity that becomes a source of leverage for further change. Anecdotally and in news reports, one hears stories about how Pope Francis's vigorous reform agenda picks up steam and soon begins to experience "push back" from some ecclesiastics who either dig in their heels or go underground waiting for more favorable times. This lack of enthusiasm for Pope Francis in some ecclesiastical quarters pales in comparison and is powerfully offset by the rising, worldwide tide of deep admiration among "ordinary" Catholics and even more generally among the people of the earth regardless of their religious preferences or lack thereof. This popularity makes the pope's assertion of a robust Vatican II reform agenda all the more irresistible.

VOCATIONAL STIRRINGS, THE JESUITS AND BEYOND

Another significant feature of Bergoglio's formative years is the exposure he had to both diocesan and religious clergy. He entered the diocesan seminary conducted by the Jesuits at Villa DeVoto, a suburb of Buenos Aires, at the age of twenty, but remained only a year and immediately switched to the Jesuit novitiate in Córdoba. As a still malleable, young seminarian in 1958, Bergoglio entered religious life at a time of extraordinary change in the Church. He entered the Jesuits during the first year of St. John XXIII's pontificate and lived through the historic, sometimes controversial changes of the Second Vatican Council as well as the initial and equally controversial adaptations of the wider Church and his Jesuit Order to the spirit of that

Council. It was a time of seemingly endless change that marked Jorge Bergoglio's earliest years in religious formation. Indeed, having finally been ordained eleven years later in 1969, he was to become the first pope whose formative years spanned this heady period of adaptation after Vatican II.

While some dispute the degree to which he "got with the project" of the Council's reforms in his early years of ministry as a priest when he was prematurely thrust into onerous leadership positions of his Jesuit province, there is no question that eventually and especially as a bishop, archbishop, and then pope, Bergoglio became convinced of the urgency of proceeding with the reforms first proposed by the Council and to do so with extraordinary courage and alacrity, with what he refers to with the Greek word taken from the Acts of the Apostles, *parrhesia*. Apropos of this, Austen Ivereigh helps clear up the ambiguity regarding Bergoglio's true vision or orientation. The British biographer explains an aspect of Bergoglio's rift with some of his Jesuit brothers in his years in the Order's leadership:

> It would be because Jorge Bergoglio clung to the idea of reform rather than rupture, of reform not revolution, that his fellow Jesuits urged Rome to name him provincial, and why he became unpopular with the avant-garde intellectuals within his province. It was they subsequently who spread the false idea of Bergoglio as a conservative, and the myth that he wanted to take the Jesuits back to before the Council. His decisions and stories tell the opposite story.[15]

At the core of this "opposite story" is Bergoglio's simple but potent missionary commitment *to engage the world as it is*, a deeply practical, pastoral option to pursue a realistic dialogue with modernity and all its various ideological offspring. The conversation must include some vexing sexual, bioethical, and ecological conundrums. Hankering over the past and turning the Church into a museum simply will not do.

While much has been written about the agitated, controversial, and even polarized years that followed the end of the Second Vatican Council, especially in Europe and the English-speaking world, the ecclesial and theological milieu of Argentina during that period remains fairly obscure. Perhaps the political situation, which was

marked by growing instability and violence, makes it hard to determine what really was happening much less know how to interpret this
lurid stretch of history. Nevertheless, this formative period in
Bergoglio's life as young priest and then as novice master and provincial of the Jesuits will arise again in the next chapter. Despite ambiguities about this controversial period of Argentine and Church
history, however, what stands out is the emergence of a gifted cohort
of thinkers and writers—some Jesuits but many diocesan priests
and laity as well, who were major players in the substantive pastoral-
theological conversations going on not only in Argentina but
throughout Latin America within the context of the Conference of
Latin American Bishops (CELAM) and the groundbreaking
Conferences of Medellín and Puebla. These events have significantly
affected the intellectual and social environment of Jorge Mario
Bergoglio. Chapter 3 takes a look at these influences in some detail.

When one looks at the socioeconomic, cultural, ecclesial, theological, and urban milieus within which Jorge Mario moved as a
gifted young *Porteño*, it becomes clear that throughout his life in one
way or another, this rich, distinctive background would exercise considerable influence on the future pope's homeland assignments and
perhaps even more so on the unfolding years of his universal ministry
in Rome. The following chapters will explore some of these earlier
experiences, others that followed, and his current conduct in many
areas of leadership. Do they bear upon his unwaveringly evangelical
and forward-looking pastoral vision?

Chapter Two

JESUIT ROOTS

Jorge Bergoglio began his life as a Jesuit on March 11, 1958, at the age of twenty-one. The early years of formation were relatively peaceful on the eve of the reforms St. John XXIII was to set in place with his call for a pastoral ecumenical council unlike any in the history of the Roman Catholic Church. As the preparations and work of the Second Vatican Council began in earnest in the early 1960s, Catholics throughout the world began to realize that this Council was going to be different. But Bergoglio's two years as a novice came a bit before this and were not yet affected by the currents of change that were soon to make themselves felt. His was a classic formation: two years as a novice followed by first vows, a year of studies in the humanities in Chile and then back to San Miguel for two years of philosophical studies and completion of his undergraduate degree. Humanly, intellectually, and spiritually speaking, what were these years like, and how did they serve as remote preparation for Jorge Mario's eventually becoming Bishop of Rome more than a half century later?

JESUIT FORMATION

Jesuit formation in those years was exceedingly uniform throughout the world. The practices of the novitiate were standard and, as could be expected, reflected the mindset of Jesuits and religious in general, which emphasized observance of the vows of poverty, chastity, and obedience. In addition, however, in the period after the restoration of the Order in the nineteenth century, the Jesuits became quite strongly rule-oriented and conservative. In 1773, the Jesuits were suppressed throughout the world except in White Russia (Poland) for rather complicated reasons. When they came back in the early nineteenth century, they were perhaps chastened and less daring than before. They no longer enjoyed the favor of monarchies and, along with the rest of the Church, were affected by the anti-Catholicism of the age of modernity and especially by the opposition and duress that the papacy itself experienced after the French Revolution, the Napoleonic invasions of the Papal States, and rising anticlericalism throughout Europe. The Jesuits of the post-restoration era, as throughout their history, were closely linked to the papacy, but in the nineteenth century and first half of the twentieth, they were more closely linked than ever. The Jesuits were among the most articulate exponents of the pope's prerogatives, and they were theological leaders at the First Vatican Council, which proclaimed the doctrine of papal infallibility. Thinking with the Church and obedience to the pope in matters pertaining to mission were undoubtedly hallmarks of the Society of Jesus when Jorge Mario Bergoglio was first attracted to the Order.[1]

Of significance was the strong humanistic orientation of Jesuit education. Bergoglio had the opportunity to read and write using some of the best examples of classical literature in Greek and Latin but also in his native Spanish and other modern European languages. His favorite poet, for instance, is the German Romantic Holderlin, and he loves opera from the days that he would listen to it on the radio with his beloved Grandma Rosa. This humanism provided him with insight into the beauty of God's creation in the humanity God loved so much and with which God identified in the incarnation. Consequently, Bergoglio is a very well-read man who taught literature at the College in Santa Fe as a young scholastic (as Jesuit seminarians are called) but, before that, had shown an interest in science, having specialized in chemistry in secondary school. His writing and speaking manifests a keen love of human knowledge in all its manifestations but especially in poetry, storytelling, and language, which he frequently uses in order to make his points. Yet he eschews anything remotely looking like snobbery or pedantry.

A current resident of Buenos Aires recalled that, as a fifteen year old student of Bergoglio's at the Jesuit Colegio de la Inmaculada Concepción in Santa Fe more than fifty years ago, he was found by Bergoglio one morning reading a huge tome titled *Sobre héroes y tumbas* (*On Heroes and Tombs*), a much-heralded but exceedingly dense and complex novel by the famous Argentine novelist Ernesto Sábato. Bergoglio asked him how he was doing and encouraged him to persevere. Decades later, when that same student, now a middle-aged man, met Ernesto Sábato himself and told him that he had read his famous novel as a fifteen year old, Sábato dismissed the experience, saying, "Fifteen year olds have no business reading my novel!" The point in recalling this story is to highlight the admiration that Bergoglio's students had in their literature teacher for his believing in them, stimulating them to inquiry, taking them serious, and respecting them, even as "mere teenagers." This anecdote shows how Bergoglio's humanistic values run deep in his personality and life, how his family set him on the right road, and how the Jesuits gave him an extraordinary context for developing his human gifts. They now have found an extraordinary place to flourish—at the pinnacle of leadership in the Church and the world.

Jesuits of Bergoglio's generation developed a clear sense of being part of a vast organization of educators and missionaries with colleges, churches, and mission posts throughout the world. Time was given to reading Jesuit history and spiritual classics. Most important, the young Jesuits were exposed to the *Spiritual Exercises* of St. Ignatius Loyola. Jesuits generally agree that what constitutes the backbone of the Jesuit way of proceeding and being has everything to do with this experience, which is fundamental for all members of the Order. The future pope's grounding in the *Spiritual Exercises*, even his expertise in them, is unquestionable. Fundamentally, the *Spiritual Exercises* are a school of prayer built around the experience of a deepening encounter with Jesus Christ and a decision to follow him in one's particular vocation throughout life.

THE DECISIVE ROLE OF THE *SPIRITUAL EXERCISES*

Around the time of Jorge Bergoglio's ordination and swift ascendency to a leadership role as novice director in 1971, Jesuits were gradually undergoing a notable renewal in their spirituality. This had to do with the retrieval of a richer, diversified approach to giving the *Spiritual Exercises*. For example, there was a move toward directed rather than preached retreats. Preached retreats consist of four or five talks per day in a large group along with assigned, common scriptures on which all the retreatants meditate several times per day. A directed retreat consists in daily personal sessions with a director or spiritual companion who may use the four weeks of the *Spiritual Exercises* as a focus or may adapt the experience to just one of the weeks or to other possibilities depending on the personal needs of the retreatant.

While this post–Vatican II renewal of the *Spiritual Exercises* was pursued with gusto throughout the Order, particularly in the United States, it influenced the practice of Ignatian spirituality in many other places as well, including Argentina. One of the consequences of the Ignatian renewal was a fuller recognition of the importance of freedom to choose one's calling based on knowledge of self and a truly personal encounter with God in Christ. The emphasis is on finding one's particular calling through getting in touch with one's deepest and most authentic desires and the cultivation of a direct relationship with God. This is where the Holy Spirit dwells in the core of one's humanity. This process requires an ability to get in touch not only with one's thoughts or intelligence but also with one's emotions. One of the consequences of this shift was a movement of Jesuits and practitioners of Ignatian spirituality away from the *ascetic* road of spirituality with its penances and numerous devotions to a more explicitly *mystical* one that emphasizes ongoing union with the triune God, "finding God in all persons and things" in daily prayer. For centuries, practitioners of the *Spiritual Exercises* had tended to reduce them to routinized practices, "canning" the experience for easy export. Yet one of the *Spiritual Exercises*' most distinctive characteristics is the use of what is called Ignatian contemplation, which requires praying with one's imagination, placing oneself in the biblical scene, using the senses of sight, touch, hearing, and even smell to evoke the encounter with the incarnate Christ. While rooted in Franciscan spirituality and popular devotion that arose in the Middle Ages, this aspect of Ignatian spirituality became suspect during the Catholic Reformation because church leaders feared that the use of the imagination in biblically based personal prayer could lead to espousing the Protestant doctrine of *sola scriptura*. The idea that one could interpret the scriptures in isolation from the rest of the ecclesial community was not the point of Ignatian contemplation, however, because such a notion fails to recognize the communal, ecclesial character of Christian spirituality and is incompatible with Catholic teaching. In the mid-twentieth century, the Jesuits were once again emphasizing the importance of the imagination in prayer, an approach that provided opportunities to discover God's presence and inspiration in one's life through memories, images, and stories that for whatever reasons may have been buried deep down in one's consciousness. As the person responsible for forming young novices in the Jesuit and Ignatian charisms, Bergoglio was surely affected by all these developments, the remarkable renewal of Ignatian spirituality over the past fifty years.[2]

If one looks even more deeply into the major dynamics of the *Spiritual Exercises*, one sees that at the heart of the process of prayer and reflection—as already noted, much of it is scripturally based—is the desire to know the person of Jesus Christ in order to willingly choose to follow him by giving one's life in service of God and neighbor in the Church. This option to follow Christ in the world is not the result of filling the mind with facts or truths about who God is on the one hand or merely tapping into one's subjectivity on the other. Rather, it is the fruit of a direct relationship with God that is experienced or lived in the *Spiritual Exercises* and beyond in a life of daily, habitual prayer. The choice to follow Christ is the result of one's own spiritual integration whereby body, mind, heart, intelligence, will, memory, and imagination are transformed by grace within the context of prayer flowing from life.

The *Spiritual Exercises* constitute a school of prayer—meditation, contemplation, and examination of consciousness, to name just a few forms of prayer found in them. Taken together, these practices of prayer can lead to a remarkably strong relationship with God in Christ and the Holy Spirit. Indeed, one might argue that the cultivation of this powerful direct relationship with God is what has often led the Jesuits and other practitioners of Ignatian spirituality to demonstrate a remarkable degree of self-possession and freedom to act, a freedom that at times may conflict with a religious mentality that emphasizes simply doing what authorities say or what the standard doctrines and rules indicate. Throughout history, Jesuits have gotten themselves into all kinds of situations and trouble demonstrating one of Bergoglio's favorite terms, "apostolic boldness" or, to use the Greek biblical term, *parrhesia*. This first referred to freedom and boldness in speech. The word is used to describe Paul's boldness before the Roman authorities and even before Peter, the head of the apostles, as reported in Galatians 2:11, where Paul says, "When Cephas (Peter) came to Antioch, I opposed him to his face, because he stood self-condemned."

The direct encounter with God so keenly fostered by the Ignatian Exercises gives depth, conviction, and assurance to those who experience it, an encounter that is qualitatively different from the indirect experience or encounter with God that Catholicism often facilitates through mediations such as the sacraments, the saints, and the Church itself. The indirect experience of God fostered in the sacraments may, of its very nature, be less personalized or motivating than an encounter one-on-one in the intimacy of prayer. The *Spiritual Exercises* are based on the assumption that this kind of personal experience is indeed possible and greatly to be pursued. The response to God's personal involvement with the one making the Exercises is a desire to act on the wonderful graces experienced by discerning God's will, to find God in all things, and a willingness, a magnanimity, to do difficult things for the sake of the gospel. In other words, the *Spiritual Exercises*, when experienced with openness and generosity, can be nothing less than dynamite. One senses that the extraordinary energy that Pope Francis is bringing to the papacy, despite his age and lung problem, flows from his sharing in the gift of a lifelong encounter with the Lord that the Ignatian Exercises have facilitated.

St. Ignatius Loyola, however, insisted on tempering this deeply personal pursuit of spiritual freedom, the discovery of one's vocation and the resulting generous response to the call of Christ the King, with an equally strong love of the larger ecclesial community, especially the hierarchical church. Ignatius had an abiding awareness of how God labors in history through limited, unworthy, and even corrupt instruments. He suffered greatly in his relationship with the papacy, which in his times, had moments of reform but often fell back into the most abysmal corruption. Indeed, before they were called Jesuits, the first name used to refer to the small band of men around St. Ignatius was "reformed priests." Ignatius is said to have had a terrible last year of life as he experienced poor health and the machinations of his many enemies in the papal court and died shortly after the elevation of his nemesis, Paul IV, to the papal throne.[3]

The ability to reconcile or integrate the Ignatian experience of spiritual freedom and a direct relationship with God with the limitations of the Church as sinful institution and its hierarchical constitution may be explained, at least in part, by the strong Christocentric orientation of the *Spiritual Exercises*. The Exercises emphasize the mystery of the incarnation: God's identification with frail humanity. A biblical and ecclesial understanding of how the Word of God, Jesus Christ, transforms the minds and hearts of the faithful requires an appreciation of what an ongoing relationship with Christ in the Spirit really entails, which is the possibility of finding God in human limitations. This means getting to know Christ as a person, as a brother and friend, an interlocutor in life's struggles, and in the confrontation with evil and pain as well as with opportunities and joys.

Father Pedro Arrupe, the late superior general of the Jesuits, discovered Bergoglio's gifts for leadership and named him novice director and, soon afterward, provincial of Argentina. Notably, Arrupe is reported to have referred to the encounter with Jesus Christ that Jesuits and others experience through the Ignatian Exercises as "falling in love."[4] This is an apt metaphor that captures the fundamentally affective and deep-seated nature of the Christian's relationship with God. Ignatian spirituality insists on the centrality of love between God and each and every one of his creatures and of those creatures with one another. It also insists that love shows itself more in actions than in words. Both the first week of the Exercises, with its meditation on the First Principle and Foundation, and the fourth and last week's Contemplation to Obtain Love emphasize the kerygmatic experience of God's unrelenting mercy and love. This is uniquely empowering, similar to the feeling that parents experience when required to act in response to threats against their children. They will confront any danger, take any risk to protect and care for them. Could this overwhelming sense of being loved by God and the resolve and power to love him in return no matter what explain the remarkable ability of Pope Francis to face many dangers and take many risks? Through the transforming power of love working in his own life in his golden years, Pope Francis has become a superman who, as it were, jumps off tall buildings and can fly! His insistence on removing the glass bubble of the popemobile, his decision not to use a bullet-proof vest, and even more telling, his courageous confrontation with elements of the Roman Curia and even the Italian mafia—all of these dramatic gestures would be mere recklessness, if they did not derive from *parrhesia*, the boldness of Christ's disciples as fostered in the Ignatian Exercises.

The Ignatian and Jesuit approach to religion and the spiritual life is profoundly holistic, insisting on the integration of all human faculties in the love affair between God and the human person. Admittedly, at first this approach may not seem truly characteristic of Jesuits and of people formed by them. The historic Jesuit commitment over the centuries to schools and the intellectual life and the intellectual accomplishments of Jesuits themselves in many fields of human inquiry may give the impression that their way of being is more cognitive than affective. The ossification of the *Spiritual Exercises* over time, the emphasis on preached retreats that repeated the same tired clichés culled from the Ignatian repertoire often forced women religious and others who were required to make annual retreats to suffer what amounted to a caricature of the Exercises. Around the time of the Second Vatican Council, however, the renewal discussed above made a big difference. Something else began to happen as laywomen and men, not only Jesuits, became proficient in giving the *Spiritual Exercises*. Consequently, in the second half of the twentieth century—the greater part of Jorge Bergoglio's active life—Ignatian spirituality had expanded its reach beyond clerics and religious as well as beyond its Western origins. This trend was certainly stronger in the Anglophone world, but it began to touch the rest of the world including Argentina in the past three decades.

IGNATIAN SPIRITUALITY AND EVANGELIZATION

It became clear that the Ignatian experience was about knowing Christ and choosing to follow him in the world, and that prayer is the key that opens this up to whomever desires to respond to this call from God. Moreover, the powerful Christocentric focus of the Ignatian Exercises correlates perfectly with the Second Vatican Council's teaching on evangelization. The building up of the Church is not so much the result of people learning more about what the Church teaches— its doctrines—as much as it is about having a personal encounter with the living God in Jesus Christ. Reason and understanding are certainly aspects of this encounter, but they are not the most important ones. Rather, as in any kind of human relationship but especially in the case of a love affair, the affective aspect is basic because that is what moves and motivates people. In other words, spirituality is about discovering that everything is a grace. This realization, more than doctrinal propositions, apologetics, cold rationality, or rules, sheds light on the real nature of the encounter with Christ that is the touchstone of Christian life. St. Paul said it all: "[He] loved me and gave himself for me" (Gal 2:20). What does one do in response to such love?

As the concept of evangelization gradually developed over the past five decades from the Second Vatican Council's *Gaudium et spes* (nos. 53ff.), Paul VI's landmark *Evangelii nuntiandi*, St. John Paul II's *Redemptoris missio*, and finally to Pope Francis's *Evangelii gaudium*, the insistence on the central role of a serious, meaningful encounter with Christ has only grown. This means that the Church's very identity and mission, which is captured best by the concept of evangelization, has brought with it a significant turn toward spirituality and pastoral care. At the heart of Christian identity is first and foremost the *kerygma*, that is, the announcement about God's reaching out to all humanity in love and mercy in the person of Jesus Christ. Doctrinal formulations, teachings, or mere ideas have their place, but they are secondary. It's not that these teachings are irrelevant, but rather that love and the entire being of the person is what is at stake in living the baptismal vocation or relationship proper to the people of God. This relates to the need for the proper disposition and attitude on the part of the evangelizer and the evangelized. To some extent, until Pope Francis came along, the persistent reference in post–Vatican II church teaching to the importance of the encounter with Christ as foundational for all evangelization seemed obscured or falsified by the sometimes obsessive interest of Rome and others in orthodoxy. Without saying so in so many words, this emphasis gave the impression that Christianity is mainly about assenting to doctrinal propositions and to moralism when, in point of fact, it is much more about "falling in love" with Christ and with the human family, Christ's brothers and sisters. Pope Francis explicitly refers to the *obsession* with doctrines, the sickness and narcissism of a self-referential church (see *Evangelii gaudium* 35).

One of the more tried and true ways of promoting the fundamentally spiritual experience of encountering Christ and thus getting out of oneself are the *Spiritual Exercises* in which Pope Francis is thoroughly grounded. Hence, this Jesuit pope has been able to move from an intellectualizing approach to teaching or magisterium, which has been typical in the post-Reformation Church and especially in the nineteenth and twentieth centuries, to one that is not nearly as conceptual. Rather, Pope Francis's teaching, like that of the *Spiritual Exercises*, gives pride of place to imagery and gesture, to imagination, memory, and emotions, and to their engagement with the broad range of human experience.

FREEDOM AND DISCERNMENT

Another powerful if not explosive ingredient of the Ignatian Exercises is the centrality they give to liberty. Indeed, at a February 2014 DePaul University conference on the new pope, Cardinal Francis George was asked what had surprised him the most about Pope Francis. He responded by saying, "His freedom."[5] The new pope demonstrated both freedom *for* and freedom *from*. Simply declining to use many of the customary trappings of the papacy from the very moment of his inauguration demonstrated a firm resolution to counteract the forces of traditionalism. Ermine capes and red shoes went out the door as did submission to the curia system that residing in the papal palace would have signaled. More significantly, on a wide range of issues from the reform of the Roman Curia to changes in the worldwide governance of the Church, Pope Francis has demonstrated in a remarkably expeditious way—for a Church that is reputed to mark change more by centuries than by years—that he is free to act and is not beholden to any particular ideological camp or interest group. Is this merely a personal quality in the man, or is it possibly linked to something more?

As commentators have observed, the cultivation of freedom is at the very core of the *Spiritual Exercises*. The title that St. Ignatius gave to his manual for spiritual development is precisely "Spiritual Exercises or How to Order Disordered Affections." The main objective of the Christian life and certainly of the life of prayer is precisely the liberty to choose to follow Christ in the world.[6] This requires the capacity to name and mitigate if not eliminate influences that drive us away from love of and service to God and neighbor—notably, the lust for power, honors, and riches. Freedom is intimately connected to discernment or what St. Ignatius calls *discrete love*. Ignatian discernment is one of the more prominent features of the Exercises, one that provides people with an often thrilling experience of being alive to God's grace because one is now freer than before from fear, prejudice, ignorance, anger, and so many other negative emotions that can undermine a creative and faithful life.[7]

The steps in the process of discernment are several. The first requires listening to one's deepest and most authentic desires, rather than covering them over with pious clichés or with what others expect of us. St. Ignatius insists on the Holy Spirit's presence within each person at the deepest recesses of his or her humanity. Ignatius asserts, as mentioned previously, a robust understanding of both God's immanence and transcendence by emphasizing the possibility of establishing a direct relationship with God. This requires both a reflective awareness of how God is present and working in one's life, especially at the levels of desire, affect, memory, and imagination (*immanence*), but also a realization of God's sovereign presence in the world and beyond (*transcendence*). The integration of God's immanence and transcendence occurs in the spiritual life in response to the experience of a personal call to follow the incarnate God/man, Jesus Christ.

Second, discipleship with Christ means striving to "get real," to be as authentic as possible, not hiding behind appearances, rank, or moralism. Third, to be in a discerning mode means becoming truly informed about the issue or decision one is considering. This demands holding knowledge and insight from whatever quarter in high regard and seeking out such knowledge. Fourth, one must consult as broadly as possible and as is necessary with others. Fifth, one must bring all this before the Lord in prayer and be sensitive to interior movements, to what gives one peace or consolation, to what agitates and inspires fear, anger, and a sense of discouragement or desolation. Persons in a discerning mode try to gain insight into their motivations, to purify them as much as possible by discovering the seeds within of self-deception, hypocrisy, and corruption. The most original spiritual practice recommended by St. Ignatius Loyola is the examen, what George Aschenbrenner calls the examination of consciousness. This is a brief, uniquely Ignatian form of prayer not to be confused with the examination of conscience before going to confession. The Ignatian examen is a handy tool by which Jesuits and others seek daily to live a more coherent discipleship of the Lord. Its key points are renewing a sense of gratitude, making gratitude one's most fundamental disposition toward life, and from that angle, looking at one's engagement with God and others, uncovering the unsavory or less worthy motivations behind our relationships and actions.[8] The gratitude one feels as a result of making the examination of consciousness a daily routine is a source of the joy of the Gospel, the disposition that Francis places above all others in reaching out to others with the good news (see *Evangelii gaudium* 2–3).

DISCERNMENT: ACTION FLOWING FROM GRATITUDE RATHER THAN FEAR

In surprising ways, Pope Francis demonstrates the various moments in the discernment process in his decision making about serious matters facing the Church. He is concerned about discernment because discernment ultimately is simple: where and how does the "rubber hit the road"? How does the Word become flesh? The survey of the Church regarding marriage and family life requested by Pope Francis in preparation for the 2014 Synod on the Family is a case in point. The survey raised a number of thorny issues such as how to respond to the sense of exclusion experienced by divorced and remarried Catholics. It requested information regarding the reception of Church teaching on contraception and same-sex marriage. In the months leading up to the first session of the Synod, these and other pastoral concerns were aired with considerable candor and in a climate of dialogue.

Regrettably, in the period after the Second Vatican Council, a kind of hermeneutic of fear that is antithetical to a truly discerning ecclesial leadership took hold. Indeed, one of the more repeated phrases in the Bible is "Fear not." Yet a fearful attitude toward the Church's engagement with the modern world became prevalent during the thirty years of the papacies of Popes John Paul II and

Benedict XVI. This is not to say that these two great churchmen had a negative impact on the Church; rather, it is to note that there was an attitude of caution during their tenure that played into the hands of restorationists and traditionalists who seemed driven by many fears and whose remedies were more like putting "new wine into old wineskins," rather than "new wine into *fresh* wineskins" (Mark 2:22). The frequent news about the investigation of theologians, the "condemnation" of Liberation Theology, the "calling on the carpet" of hundreds of theologians by the Congregation of the Doctrine of the Faith headed by Cardinal Ratzinger for more than two decades created a climate of fear and a discouragement of serious discussion that delayed open debate about pressing issues of pastoral and moral concern. In contrast, Pope Francis's approach is more clearly in continuity with the orientation of the majority at the Second Vatican Council, which insisted on the need to engage the world, not retreat from it. Nevertheless, it would be unfair to conclude that either Pope John Paul II or Pope Benedict XVI did not also make extraordinary contributions to the Church's dialogue with the world. Yet it is undeniable that, for whatever reasons, a climate of suspicion and fear did take hold of Catholics and contributed to what Pope Francis perceptively identified as a self-referential, narcissistic Church. A fearful attitude was nurtured by the rhetoric of culture wars that some church leaders used to exploit terms like the "culture of death" in the papal magisterium to advance their ideologies and justify policies of caution and suspicion in the very heart of the Church. In this process, the Church became, to use Pope Francis's word, "sick." The Catholic Church, nevertheless, owes Pope Benedict XVI a profound debt of gratitude because he realized that serious reform at several levels was necessary, and he stepped aside in order to create the conditions for such a reform. Arguably, his resignation will be heralded as a turning point in the worldwide direction of the Church because it opened the way for the coming of Pope Francis.

A rather notable feature of Pope Francis's Petrine ministry is his predilection for the teachings of Pope Paul VI. To some extent, it is as if Pope Francis emphasizes the Second Vatican Council's call for reading the signs of the times and its repeated calls for reform that came to a head during Pope Paul VI's papacy. It is significant that Pope Francis insists that Pope Paul VI's *Evangelii nuntiandi* is "the post-conciliar document that is yet to be surpassed."[9] Pope Francis wants to focus on Pope Paul's and the Second Vatican Council's unfinished business. In pursuit of this goal, Pope Francis takes to discernment more readily in that he exhibits the antecedent freedom that is always necessary for decision making. In the lead-up to making a decision, time is needed to air different points of view. There is no question that Pope Francis has considerably improved the climate around decision making and dialogue among parties with differing opinions. His approach favors putting the issues on the table and discussing them from every angle. This contrasts with an approach that either explicitly or by inference takes certain topics off the table. In some areas, for example, in regard to abortion or same-sex marriage, Pope Francis has indicated that the conversation is closed. In many areas, however, he has created an atmosphere of intense engagement with reality on the ground and generated an ongoing discussion about possible pastoral approaches, for example, the dialogue among bishops, cardinals, and theologians about divorced and remarried Catholics or the pastoral care of gay, Lesbian, and transsexual persons.

IGNATIAN PRAYER

The Extraordinary Synod on the Family in October 2014 provided an excellent example of how the reform of Pope Francis is introducing elements of Ignatian discernment into matters of ecclesial reform. One of the elements is simply openness, being open to the propositions of others as recommended by St. Ignatius in number 22 of the *Spiritual Exercises*. This means fostering an approach that does not begin by setting down clear parameters or "lines in the sand." Rather, this method requires the ability to listen. Despite the fact that in regard to the issue of women priests, no change in the position of Pope John Paul II has occurred under Pope Francis, in other significant areas, nevertheless, new ways of thinking have emerged about delicate issues such as cohabitation, same-sex marriage, and communion for divorced and remarried Catholics who have not obtained an annulment. By the same token, Francis has highlighted critical aspects of Catholic social teaching on the economy with his insistent call for concern for the poor, thus bringing into play more than ever the developing world's perspectives into the very heart of the global Church. In so many of his words and actions, Pope Francis reveals his grounding in the Jesuit way of proceeding and the underlying spirituality that gives serious attention to discernment based on solid information. This is seen, for example, in the case of social policy regarding the extreme socioeconomic inequality that afflicts the world today. The focus on analysis of reality, contemplation in action, and paying attention to what is, is one of the signature qualities of this pope and of his deep Ignatian heritage.

Chapter Three

THE LATIN AMERICAN
ETHOS OF RENEWAL

The reception given the Second Vatican Council in Latin America was substantive, and that region's response to the Council's message of reform was arguably the most robust and creative of any region of the world.[1] In 1965, on their return from Rome at the end of the Council, a solid core of extraordinarily gifted churchmen—the Brazilian, Helder Camara; the Chilean, Manuel Larraín; and the Argentine, Eduardo Pironio, to name just a few—had the benefit of the unprecedented infrastructure of the Latin American Conference of Bishops, known as CELAM, to collaborate in forging a renewed ecclesial vision adapted to the reality of Latin America. Indeed, Bishops Manuel Larraín and Helder Camara had both served as founding fathers of CELAM in the 1950s. CELAM became a fertile, creative source of pastoral-theological vision throughout the second half of the twentieth century and into the twenty-first. Eduardo Pironio, a protégé of Pope Paul VI, who served as rector of the Catholic University of Argentina in the 1960s, became a conduit to Rome of Latin American concerns and initiatives on behalf of economic justice for all and for seminal concepts like "option for the poor" and base ecclesial communities. Pironio was a classmate of Cardinal Antonio Quarracino, who decades later selected Jorge Mario Bergoglio as his auxiliary bishop and then got Bergoglio promoted to replace him as archbishop on retirement. Pope Francis is linked in many ways with some of the more outstanding lights of the renewal of the Church in Latin America, especially with Cardinal Pironio, the friend of Bergoglio's principal supporter and mentor, Quarrancino.

THE INFLUENCE OF HELDER CAMARA AND CELAM

Nowhere else in the world did a regional gathering of bishops have such an active regional organization as CELAM anticipating the movement toward synodality and collegiality first suggested by the Second Vatican Council and later championed by Pope Francis. Perhaps CELAM, more than any other source, has contributed to the rise of a new and exciting vision for the Church in Latin America and beyond. This is the vision in which Bergoglio was steeped during his most impressionable years as a young Jesuit but also later as provincial, bishop, and archbishop. CELAM has been the driving force behind a continuous and coherent process of theological reflection and pastoral action from 1955 at its inception in Rio de Janeiro to the present. With headquarters in Bogotá, CELAM has provided a space for the development of vibrant and ongoing theological reflection that has been renewed over the decades by four impressive, hemispheric gatherings of the bishops of Latin America and the Caribbean—by far the largest gathering of regional bishops in the world. CELAM was the brainchild of Dom Helder Camara, who first served the National Conference of Brazilian Bishops (CNBB) as Secretary General from its inception in 1952 until 1964. Interestingly, Dom Helder got to know Monsignor Giovanni Battista Montini, the future Pope Paul VI, in the early 1950s. Montini was a source of considerable support for Dom Helder in his work at the CNBB and then in the founding of CELAM. Dom Helder died in 1999 after retirement as Archbishop of Recife-Olinda in Northeast Brazil.

There are interesting points of comparison between Pope Francis and the earlier Dom Helder. For one thing, both experienced strong interests in social, economic, and political change. At one point in the 1940s, Dom Elder was strongly attracted to politics, but in his case, to anticommunism. As a matter of fact, he identified with a political movement that was considered fascist. Certainly, it was populist and reflected the visions of contemporary rightist Catholic political movements in Spain, Italy, and Argentina. Brazil had its own populist, Getulio Vargas, who led Brazil as president, first as dictator and then as democratically elected, for longer than any other figure in that nation's history with the exception of the nineteenth-century

Emperor Pedro II. Interestingly, as a young man, Dom Helder was attracted to the anticommunism of Vargas's party, his ability to integrate principles from Catholic social teaching into the political agenda, and his inspiring populism. Later in life, after Dom Helder had rejected anything related to fascism and became a champion of the poor in the spirit of Liberation Theology, these early associations with Vargas's politics were used against him by his detractors, among whom were some Brazilian and other Latin American bishops. They also attacked his shift toward more leftist positions. Indeed, he was known by some as the "Red Bishop."

Dom Helder had a personal style of speaking and living somewhat reminiscent of Jorge Bergoglio. He eschewed ecclesiastical ostentation, dressed as simply as possible, and lived in a very modest dwelling. He created more than a little animosity among some bishops who felt he was calling their lavish and pompous ways into question, which of course he was. The 1970s and '80s was a period of bitter recriminations in response to chronic unrest and violence that included some persecution of clerics and even bishops who clearly sided with the poor and were accused of coddling the Marxists. Dom Helder emerged as a lightning rod in support of the fuller implications of "the preferential option for the poor" adopted by the body of bishops in their hemispheric conferences of Medellín and Puebla. He remained controversial to the very end.[2]

Jorge Bergoglio's formation years for the Jesuit priesthood corresponded to these exhilarating, conflictual, and heady times of change initiated by the Second Vatican Council as well as by the Cold War, various postcolonial movements, and rising unrest in Central America, Brazil, Chile, Argentina, and other Latin American hotspots. Of particular relevance for understanding Bergoglio is the way in which this period unfolded in Argentina, especially in terms of renewal and change in the local Church.

THE ARGENTINE RESPONSE TO VATICAN II

In 1966, the Argentine bishops established the Episcopal Commission on Pastoral Care (*Comisión Episcopal de Pastoral*) known by its abbreviation COEPAL. The purpose of COEPAL was to develop a pastoral plan for Argentina based on the pastoral vision of the Second Vatican Council, particularly *Gaudium et spes* and *Lumen gentium*. The importance given to pastoral planning was totally in line with the pastoral-theological bent of the Council, which emphasized a specific methodology proposed for the Church, dioceses, parishes, and other Catholic organizations, namely, one that proceeded in an *inductive* rather than *deductive* manner. The seeds for such an inductive methodology begin with an analysis of reality, getting in touch with the concrete situation of one's people, parish, diocese, region, or nation. In this, the human sciences—anthropology, sociology, political science, economics, and history—played an important role.

This approach of course was first implemented in the pre–Vatican II era under the inspiration of Cardinal Joseph Cardijn's well-known "see-judge-act" methodology that has come to be called the pastoral circle.[3] This way of proceeding inspired a generation of Catholic thinkers and activists in Europe, Latin America, and the United States in the third and fourth decades of the twentieth century. Interestingly, Bishop Larraín was trained in this methodology by Cardinal Joseph Cardijn's powerfully motivating Young Christian Workers known as the "Jocist" movement for its name in Spanish. Similarly, the revered Chilean Jesuit, St. Alberto Hurtado, a colleague of Larraín's, was definitely inspired by the Jocist movement. Bergoglio knew of St. Alberto, who died in 1952 and had lived and worked in the very house of studies outside Santiago, where Bergoglio did a year of studies in humanities in 1960.

ARGENTINE INFLUENCES

Two outstanding Argentine theologians who were active in COEPAL arose in the first half of the twentieth century and especially at the time of Vatican II, Lucio Gera (1924–2012) and Rafael Tello (1917–2002). These two extraordinary teachers are arguably among the most significant Argentine theologians of this period and contributed more than any others to the theological landscape of Jorge Mario Bergoglio. They are key players in the theological-pastoral vision of the 266th pope. Along with them, Juan Luis Scannone must also be mentioned as one of the more accomplished Argentine philosophers/theologians and Catholic writers of the second half of the twentieth century and first decades of the twenty-first. A few years older than Bergoglio and one of his teachers, Scannone along with Carlos María Galli, who wrote a dissertation at the Catholic University of Argentina on Lucio Gera, are probably the most knowledgeable scholars regarding the intellectual and pastoral formation of Bergoglio within the rich, dramatic, theological environment of the times.

The establishment of COEPAL in the wake of Vatican II and the Medellín Conference set in motion the distinctive pastoral vision that would emerge fifty years later on the world scene as "the Francis effect." Among the activities of COEPAL was the adaptation of the directives and vision of the 1968 Medellín Conference of CELAM to the Argentine Church. Lucio Gera was a consultant and writer for the Medellín conference and later for the Puebla Conference of 1979. He and Tello were also important players in a 1968 conference convened by the Argentine bishops at San Miguel, the location of the Jesuit Colegio Máximo where Bergoglio was contemporaneously studying theology in preparation for ordination. The resulting *Document of San Miguel* (DSM) serves as an anchor for the developments in pastoral care and methods of the following decades in Argentina. These were precisely the years that marked the meteoric rise of Jorge Mario Bergoglio, first within the Society of Jesus and then within the wider Church in Argentina.

LUCIO GERA

At this point, it makes sense to step back a little to profile the factors that contributed to the intense pastoral-theological ethos that powerfully informed the future pope's formation and mature years as Jesuit and bishop. Some outstanding players in this process of creating the distinctive ecclesial and theological ecology of Jorge Bergoglio's Argentina as already mentioned were two diocesan priests, Lucio Gera and Rafael Tello. Like Jorge Bergoglio's father Mario, Lucio Gera came to Argentina from Italy in the 1920s—but much younger—as a five year old child. He enjoyed a long, productive life as revered priest, pastor, teacher, and theological writer. Gera was an intellectual and a front-row player in many events that affected the Church during his long life. Theologian Virginia Azcuy summarizes his vast accomplishments in the following way:

Without exaggerating one can say that his history reveals and speaks about the realism of God's coming into this world in the flesh, and of the gift that the Church is for humanity, and of the absolute destiny that unfolds in the pilgrimage of peoples and their cultures.[4]

The key words here are *realism, humanity,* and *pilgrimage.* They echo strongly today in Papa Bergoglio's Gospel-inspired vision for the Church. Cardinal Bergoglio thought so highly of Gera that, on his death in 2012, he insisted that Gera be buried in the crypt of the archbishops of Buenos Aires. Who was he?

Gera was a systematic theologian who took the pastoral-practical purpose of theology extremely seriously. From the very outset of the post–Vatican II era, he played a central role in the conversations and theological products of the Church in both Latin America and Argentina. He was both a consultant and writer for the General Conferences of Medellín and Puebla. He served in the same capacity for the trend-setting San Miguel Conference of Argentine Bishops in 1969. He was named to the International Theological Commission by Pope Paul VI in that same year. Moreover, Gera held key teaching and administrative positions at the Catholic University of Argentina (CUA). Like other players in this unfolding period of ecclesial ferment, Gera had been deeply invested in the Young Christian Workers or Jocist movement in his younger years. He wrote for the Jocist journal *Notas de Pastoral Jocista.* Already, the themes that would occupy a lifetime and serve as focus for Jorge Bergoglio's pastoral vision were in gestation in Gera's teaching and writing: workers' issues, the poor and the beatitudes, and the inculturation of the faith in the popular culture of Argentina and Latin America. In the 1970s, Gera was part of the influential COEPAL committee and contributed to the *Document of San Miguel,* especially section VI, which treats the theme of popular piety. The document serves as the foundational statement of pastoral vision for post–Vatican II Argentina even though, in the give and take of the intervening years, its focus on reform was muted by the resistance of bishops, chronic political crises, and internecine violence.

Among Gera's most productive years were the 1970s and '80s despite the terrible political persecutions of the military dictatorship.

Working in tandem with him was a group of theologians and other academics in the field of social sciences and philosophy. They created what was called the *Cátedras Nacionales de Sociología*, centers for social science analysis. Speaking of a synergy that developed between Gera's theological group and the *Cátedras Nacionales* social science cohort, Scannone observes that both groups distanced themselves from both capitalism and Marxism. Moreover, they "found their conceptualization in Latin American and Argentine history (real and written) with categories like 'people,' and 'antipeople,' and 'peoples contrasted with empires,' and 'popular culture,' and 'popular religiosity.'"[5] In fact, Gera collaborated in the production of what has been called *La Teología del Pueblo*, which arose contemporaneously with Liberation Theology as a theological method that served the changing reality of the Church in Latin America first by requiring church leadership to pay close attention to the concrete situation on the ground. Like Liberation Theology, this Argentine version gave pride of place to induction rather than deduction. It preferred to correlate the reality of the community as elucidated and grasped in history and the social sciences with the sources of Christian faith, that is, with Sacred Scripture, Tradition, and the Church's official teaching—the magisterium, as it is called.[6] History and cultural anthropology became the particular lenses through which Gera and his contemporary, Rafael Tello, reflected on the challenges posed to the Church's pastoral praxis by historical developments in the second half of the twentieth century, decades marked by severe sociopolitical and ecclesial tensions.

Gera exercised great influence for decades through his service on commissions of CELAM. He contributed to the final documents of both Medellín and Puebla. He and Tello, more than any other Latin American theologians of the time, insisted on the central importance of *religiosidad popular*, the faith of the ordinary believer as expressed in popular piety. They gave much more importance to historical and cultural analysis than to Marxist-inspired socioeconomic analysis. Moreover, they both suggested that popular culture, including popular religion, constitutes the most important field for sowing the word of God for evangelization. It is said that Gera wrote the salient paragraphs of the *Document of Puebla* (nos. 444–69), which give even more importance than the *Document of Medellín* to the people's religion. He linked popular piety to the ancient doctrine of the *sensus fidei*, which affirms the presence of the Holy Spirit in the faithful intuitions of all the baptized. These distinctive emphases capture the nature of the difference between liberation theologians, who viewed popular piety with skepticism as alienating and, as Marx contended, the "opium of the people," and others like Gera and his Argentine school of thought, which hailed the faith of the people as the desired product of the encounter of the Gospel with the culture of real, ordinary people. As Austen Ivereigh points out, Gera insisted on this key principle, namely that "the activity of the Church should not only be oriented toward the people but also primarily derive *from* the people."[7] This principle has worked its way directly into the major teachings of Pope Francis's pontificate, most notably in *Evangelii gaudium*, where we read the following:

> Each portion of the people of God, by translating the gift of God into its own life and in accordance with its own genius, bears witness to the faith it has received and enriches it with new and eloquent expressions. One can say that a "people continuously evangelizes itself." Herein lies the importance of popular piety, a true expression of the spontaneous missionary activity of the people of God. This is an ongoing and developing process of which the Holy Spirit is the principal agent. (no. 122)

While remaining in dialogue with other committed Latin American theologians, it is undeniable that Gera, Tello, and several others among the Argentine theological leadership did not share the tendency of some of their Latin American colleagues to adopt the modernity of either Marxism or Western liberalism. That is why Gera and *La Teología del Pueblo* rejected the method of socioeconomic analysis preferred by Marxism as well as the analyses of Western Enlightenment culture in both its continental and Anglo-Saxon forms. Gera explicitly referred to Enlightenment culture as a threat. Early on, Gera pointed out that there are two great threats to the integrity of the faith of the Latin American peoples. The first originated in the European Enlightenment as it was advanced by the Bourbon monarchs of the eighteen century, giving rise to the liberal elites of the independence period of the nineteenth century in Latin

America. The second was the highly influential version of Enlightenment culture that was fed by the distinctive, Anglo Saxon current propagated by the newly established United States of America with its emphasis on democracy and egalitarianism. Writing in the 1980s, Gera claimed that Enlightenment culture is

> the principal contradiction and threat currently experienced by Latin America, a contradiction that puts enlightenment culture in opposition to its own (Latin American) culture, even more than other contradictions, for instance that between white European cultures and the indigenous ones.[8]

Gera's approach to theological method gives special importance to the faith of the people. Rather than paying attention to socioeconomic factors, Gera highlights the role of popular culture in its anthropological sense as the locus of meaning for the way of thinking, feeling, and being of an entire people. For him, the challenge of pastoral care revolves around an honest confrontation with the people's reality. Preconceived ideological frameworks and even doctrinal formulations can interfere in this process. This also requires that pastoral ministers possess a sense of history because the people's faith is lived in time and can either freeze at moments of paralysis and malaise or move forward dynamically under the inspiration of the Holy Spirit.[9]

Moreover, the *people* are the protagonists of the Church's evangelizing mission, and their way of being Church, interestingly, contrasts in significant ways with what the hierarchical, clerical Church understands by Church. Indeed, it is crucial that the Church's official teachers grasp the significance of what it means to truly be a people. For the Church is "a people." Gera puts it this way:

> The poor person ultimately implies a moral condition whose basic characteristic is *humble openness toward others*, God and mankind. "Thirst for God, is something that only the poor and simple can know" according to Pope Paul VI in *Evangelii nuntiandi*, No. 48. The experience of not having power leads the poor to feel the need for others, to

request, plead and demand of others the justice and affection they require. The *first condition for really belonging to a people is the awareness of needing others*, and this is in a poor person a live, inherited awareness. That is why of his or her nature a poor person is more capable of experiencing solidarity—giving to others and expecting something in return, more capable of "being in a people." Because by "people" is meant something really ethical that demands profound moral attitudes. Thus without a doubt we preferentially refer to the multitude of poor persons as "the people."[10]

When Pope Francis repeats St. John XXIII's call for a "poor Church for the poor," he is making the point that the Church exists for the people. In Latin America and certainly throughout the world with some exceptions, of course, the people to whom the Church is called to reach out and serve are quite literally the poor, for they constitute the majority of human beings on the planet. Even more, the principal agents of evangelization are these people whose popular culture, not the enlightened culture of the Western world nor even the Church's own ecclesiastical culture, constitutes the locus—the place—where faith and culture are primarily encountered and gestated. While the theological concept of people of God—all the baptized—is not the same as people, yet the people of God exercise their evangelizing mission within the larger context of the "people." Consequently, the pivotal role Gera gives to the concept of people cannot be overemphasized. The values, ways of being, thinking, and feeling that constitute a "people" are precisely the values, ways of being, thinking, and feeling that are the targets of the Church's mission to evangelize. Pope Francis's frequent reference to the *pueblo fiel de Dios* (faithful people of God) demonstrates the influence that *Lumen gentium*'s ecclesiology of the people of God has on him, but beyond that, it reflects the distinctive approach to the broader category of "people" in Gera's thought as well as in that of Gera's colleague Rafael Tello to be discussed in chapter 4.

Austen Ivereigh reports that, as provincial in 1974, Bergoglio gave a retreat to a school faculty and staff at which he explained how it is that Christian hope is incarnate in the "ordinary non-enlightened

Argentine *pueblo fiel* rather than in the enlightened elites who grav-
itate more toward ideology than Christian hope.[11] The concept of
"people" as understood by Gera and Tello is consequently a key for
understanding several themes in Pope Francis's teaching. It relates to
the persistent concern he has for ideology, ideas, and even doctrines
overpowering a common sense, pastoral regard for the facts on the
ground, for reality. It also helps explain his enthusiasm for the teaching of the *Concluding Document of Aparecida* regarding the call to missionary discipleship as fundamental for all the baptized, thus insisting
on the *agency of all believers* as a counterweight to the ecclesiastical
tendency to concentrate leadership in the hands of clerical or religious
elites. The faithful are called to be protagonists, not mere spectators.

In connection with this, Gera and Tello help clarify something
that is rather obvious. In the conduct of Pope Francis in the first
years of his pontificate, the Argentine pope has become an implaca-
ble critic of *ecclesiastical* culture. For, in Gera's and Tello's scheme of
things, it is not only enlightened culture that is an enemy of the
people's vocation as principal evangelizers. Indeed, ecclesiastical culture in the form of clericalism and "spiritual worldliness" directly
contradicts the Church's mission to evangelize and constitutes a perpetual "elephant" in Holy Mother Church's living room. To adequately grasp Tello's contribution to the fascinating theological ethos
of Jorge Bergoglio's Argentina, the works of Enrique Ciro Bianchi
and Omar César Albado are most illuminating.

In 2012, Bianchi published his doctoral thesis on Rafael Tello,
and Cardinal Jorge Bergoglio was kind enough to write the prologue
for this engrossing study. The future pope begins by stating that the
book "connects us to the life and thought of someone who was one of
the most brilliant minds of the Argentine Church in the twentieth
century." He goes on to say that Tello had a rich personality and did
many things during his lifetime. Bianchi's book, Bergoglio tells us, is
a great introduction to this singular thinker and to his novel theological views. In a description of Tello's thinking that today would serve
just as well as a fundamental statement of what he would be about as
pope, Bergoglio said that

> Tello was a theologian and pastor taken up with love of
> God, of the Virgin Mary and of his people. He had a

passion for history and for offering his time, heart, and intelligence to the poor. His theology prophetically points to our poorest brothers and sisters. He reminds us that they are in the center of God's heart so much so that Christ made himself poor. His theology motivates us to ask whether we give to the poor the place they deserve. It invites us to transform the Church into the house of the poor.[12]

The future pope also insisted on Tello's creativity and fidelity to sound Church teaching, which explains the profound influence of his thoughts on the *Concluding Document of Aparecida*. As a result of Aparecida's recognition of the central importance of popular piety—something that Tello advanced his entire life—Bergoglio notes the following:

After Aparecida, popular piety can no longer be treated as the Cinderella of the house. It is not just a matter of tolerating popular religious expressions; rather, it is about strengthening in its own ways what constitutes a true, popular form of spirituality.[13]

Thus the significant contribution of Tello's theology to the Argentine pope's thinking needs further elaboration. Tello's thoughts are complex and quite original. Given the obvious regard that Jorge Bergoglio has for Tello's theological contributions, the following chapter will explore this remarkable but obscure Argentine theologian at greater length.

Chapter Four

RAFAEL TELLO AND THE FAITHFUL PEOPLE OF GOD

In the prologue to Enrique Ciro Bianchi's study of the thought of Rafael Tello, Cardinal Bergoglio refers to the great master, Tello, as "a theologian and pastor taken up by the love of God, of the Virgin Mary and of his people."[1] Tello's passion and his whole being, the cardinal tells us, was totally focused on the poor and on the Church's prophetic mission. Such a theology raises the question as to whether the poor are receiving the attention they rightly deserve, whether the Church really is the *casa de los pobres* (house of the poor). Reading Bergoglio's encomium of Tello, one is reminded of Bergoglio's own predilection for the poor, one well known in Buenos Aires but generally hidden from view from the rest of the world until Bergoglio's dramatic and unexpected appearance on the global scene. Might not the very same observation Bergoglio makes about Tello be made about Bergoglio himself who wrote that "Fr. Tello's life was a gift of the Holy Spirit to our Church. His creativity was unequaled."[2]

Who was this Tello with whom Bergoglio enjoys a profound spiritual and theological kinship? His story is actually rather remarkable and somewhat unusual. Tello was unquestionably a teacher, writer, and thinker who exercised a great influence over a generation or two of Argentine church leaders. Tello's life and work are still quite obscure due to the fact that very little of his theological writings and teachings were ever published, and he spent decades in relative seclusion before his death in 2002.

That is all changing, however. The Saracho Foundation was established to disseminate his work, and several books have appeared in the last five years. The first book-length effort to get at the core thought of Tello is Bianchi's *Pobres en este Mundo, Ricos en la Fe* (Poor in This World, Rich in Faith), published in 2012. In addition to Bianchi, there are three other theologians who have written about Tello: Víctor Manuel Fernández, Marcelo González, and Omar Albado. It deserves notice that Fernández, as already mentioned, belongs to the inner circle of Pope Francis's theological confidants. By all reports, Fernández is the closest theologian to Pope Francis and reputed to be one of the main contributors to *Evangelii gaudium*.[3] This connection only reinforces the suspicion that Tello may indeed be an important source of theological inspiration, perhaps a key source for Bergoglio's pastoral-theological vision.

TELLO'S LIFE

Tello was born in the city of La Plata just south of Buenos Aires in 1917. His family had land in the extreme northwestern Argentine province of Jujuy, where he spent many vacations and family visits as a youth. This is significant because this exposed Tello at a formative time of life to the "other" Argentina, the mestizo one far to the north, whose people included descendants of the great indigenous civilizations of the Andes that rise rapidly starting in Jujuy. This region pertained to the original colonial jurisdiction of the viceroyalty of Lima far to the north, which was the seat of government for Argentina until the eighteenth century when the viceroyalty of La Plata was established. In boyhood experiences in this place, so decidedly different from what he knew in greater Buenos Aires, Tello gained a deep sense of the contrast between cultures—urban, rural, European, and indigenous—as well as direct knowledge of social class differences.

At the age of twenty-seven, Tello became a lawyer. At this time, he was active in Catholic Action and Young Christian Workers at his parish and among university students whom he served as an adviser. He entered the seminary in 1945 and was ordained five years later. In 1958, he became a professor of theology at the Theological Faculty of Buenos Aires. From 1966 to 1973, he was a consultant for COEPAL, as mentioned above, a seminal hothouse of pastoral-theological visions and initiatives for the Argentine bishops, inspired on the exciting events of Vatican II and the Medellín Conference. In addition, Tello, like Gera, was actively engaged with many priests in the controversial Movement of Priests for the Third World. This organization was soon characterized as more than a little sympathetic to Marxist ideology. In the period of the generals, it was persecuted and Bergoglio, now serving as Jesuit provincial, certainly tried to keep his distance from it, since it was considered a source of intellectual and spiritual inspiration for the Montoneros, the radical, left-wing guerilla movement that struggled against the military dictatorship's national security state in the 1970s. Tello was certainly not a Marxist sympathizer, but he was a critic of capitalism in conformity with Catholic social teaching. Moreover, Bergoglio was and remains today deeply committed to social change within the framework of that same teaching.

Father Tello's active life as a priest lasted from 1950 to 1979. For the next twenty-three years until his death in 2002, Tello went into voluntary seclusion and quite literally ostracized himself from the public exercise of the priesthood. No clear explanation was ever given regarding his decision to do so, but it seems to have had to do with serious differences he had with his Archbishop Juan Carlos Aramburu.[4] He resigned his position in the theological faculty and went to live in his family home. From there, he remained in contact with many priests, religious, and lay ecclesial leaders. He would give workshops on faith and culture, evangelization, and popular piety for small groups of priest friends and others who would come to hear him, take notes, and receive his counsel. Many of his talks were taped, and some of his students printed summaries of his teaching taken from notes, which were then circulated.

Tello remained a somewhat controversial figure in political circles in that he had been identified with the Movement of Priests for the Third World, but after the disaster of the military dictatorship and the hopeless war of the generals with Great Britain over the Malvinas (commonly called the Falkland Islands in English), the political climate changed and suspicions against the generals' opponents declined. During his years of reclusion, Tello helped found three thriving organizations. The first is an association of the faithful called Holy Mary, Star of Evangelization, which is also known as the Confraternity of the Virgin of Luján. A second association is called "Negrito Manuel," which refers to the African slave involved in the narrative about the miracle of Our Lady of Luján to which the most popular shrine in Argentina is dedicated. Today, people who make outstanding contributions in the field of communications media in Argentina are honored annually with the Negrito Manuel Award—similar to the Oscar or the Emmy in the United States. The third organization is the Saracho Foundation, which is committed to the study and promotion of popular Argentine and Latin American cultures as a vehicle for the Church's evangelizing mission. It does this through publications, cultural events, and a substantial Web site.

TELLO'S THOUGHTS

In the effort to identify sources of inspiration for Jorge Bergoglio during the intense period of church renewal and dangers in Argentina during the past four decades, the influence exercised by Tello on the development of popular devotion in Argentina is notable. There are two intensely popular and profoundly significant *santuarios* in the Buenos Aires area: San Cayetano de Liniers and Nuestra Señora de Luján. Tello contributed to a change of focus—perhaps one could say a "remarketing"—for both sanctuaries that occurred in the 1970s. The changes had to do with the integration of sociopolitical with devotional concerns. In other places in Latin America, for example, Central America, Brazil, or Peru, new cohorts of theologians identified with the Second Vatican Council's call for social justice and initially interpreted the reality of oppression in a way that emphasized practical rationality. These theologians gave pride of place to a moral and ethical stance grounded in an intellectual discourse, an analysis of reality, at home in the modern world.

This modern discourse often takes the form of either Marxism or liberalism. Liberalism, in this context, does not mean, as in the United States, left-leaning politics, but rather free-market capitalism. In Latin America, undoubtedly, there was considerable sympathy for various socialist or Marxist interpretations of socioeconomic reality and deep-seated antipathy for capitalist or what is called in many parts of the world neo-liberal ideology. In connection with this, popular piety was often critiqued by Catholic leaders themselves (not just Marxists or secularists) as alienating or, more often, benignly neglected. The Catholic leadership that identified with sociopolitical change sometimes threw its lot in with revolutionary forces that took up arms. This does not refer, of course, to Archbishop Oscar Romero or the vast majority of other martyrs produced during that bloody period. Nevertheless, there was considerable ambiguity about the legitimacy and effectiveness of resorting to violence for the sake of overcoming oppression under the concrete circumstances of the revolutionary movements in the 1970s and '80s throughout Latin America. The Cold War complicated matters and made it difficult for some to distinguish between the struggle for justice and sympathy with international communism.

In sharp contrast to these developments, Tello, together with Lucio Gera and many other Argentine Catholics, took another tack. They seized on the remarkable phenomena of the sanctuaries of San Cayetano and Luján to forge a distinctively Latin American, Catholic integration of religious fervor and spirituality with a direct, graphic, and compelling response to the reality of poverty and injustice—an explicitly nonviolent and non-Marxist one. Moreover, this response took seriously a principle that Tello expressed repeatedly in his teaching and writing—namely, the most suitable vehicle for the Church's identity and evangelizing mission in Latin America and, by inference, beyond, is popular culture. True evangelization must first come *desde* or "*from*" the people. Anything that smacks of arm-chair ideology of the right or the left is rejected. Popular culture, according to Tello, knows how to integrate the pursuit of material and social needs with *mística*, a blend of popular religion, spirituality, and mysticism. A simple visit to the Web sites of the Santuario of San Cayetano and of Our Lady of Luján today reveals the distinctive character of these places of devotion and pilgrimage decades later. They are at once expressions of the community's deep piety and faith, especially of the most needy, but also impressive instruments of social service where food, clothing, housing, and medical needs are readily available. Nor are they merely concerned with charity but also with advocacy and even empowerment of the community. They serve as centers of political (but not partisan) mobilization. Accordingly, the way to go about abetting social awareness and action is suggested by the popular solidarity expressed in customs, rituals, art, and music of the community itself rather than by the cold, rationalist pragmatism and vanguardism of modern political and intellectual elites.

Omar Albado helps one understand what is behind the remarkable phenomena of Lujan and San Cayetano. He has brilliantly synthesized Tello's theology by pointing out how his focus on popular culture is the result of his conviction that the Church cannot accomplish its purpose without "turning to the concrete human person."[5] In Tello's *La Teología del Pueblo*, one finds the theological warrant for such a necessity. Tello proposes first of all that this turn to the concrete human person is a doctrinal thread throughout the documents of the Second Vatican Council, especially *Gaudium et spes*. As a matter of fact, St. John Paul II picked up this notion and made it a source of inspiration for three of his major works: *Redemptoris hominis*, *Dives in misericordia*, and *Tertio millennio adveniente*. John Paul asserts the centrality of the human person without mincing words when he writes that "for the Church all ways lead to man" (*Redemptoris hominis* 14). Tello builds on this simple but bold assertion of Christian anthropology in *Fundamentos de una Nueva Evangelización* (Foundations of a New Evangelization), where he points out that a central concern of the Second Vatican Council was to clearly assert an ecclesiology that conceives of the Church's identity as a mission centered on the existential, concrete human person as he or she is found in the real world. Tello tells us that the target of the Church's activity is

> not an abstract person, considered as some idea or conception about what he or she is, or viewed in terms of his or her nature (which would still be just an abstraction), but rather a concrete person born of woman, created by God and called by Him to participate in his life which is eternal. Consequently, the object of the Church's care is the entire human person, in all his or her dimensions—eternal, temporal, spiritual and corporal, individual and communitarian —*all* persons and *each one* of them.[6]

This turn toward the human person, however, is not simply some exalted form of humanism or anthropocentrism. There is a clear hierarchy of doctrine here that insists on God having the place of honor, followed by Christ the redeemer, then by the Church as instrument of God's reign, and finally focused on each and every human person. In this "incarnational" scheme, a God both transcendent and immanent

is decidedly at the heart of the Church's mission. Tello goes on to cite
St. John Paul II's *Dives in misericordia*:

> The more the Church's mission is centered upon man—
> the more it is, so to speak, anthropocentric—the more it
> must be confirmed and actualized theocentrically, that is
> to say, be directed in Jesus Christ to the Father. While the
> various currents of human thought both in the past and at
> the present have tended and still tend to separate theocen-
> trism and anthropocentrism, and even to set them in
> opposition to each other, the Church, following Christ,
> seeks to link them up in human history, in a deep and
> organic way. And this is also one of the basic principles,
> perhaps the most important one, of the teaching of the last
> Council. (no. 1)

The thrust of Tello's thinking goes in the direction of popular culture,
especially what he calls *pastoral popular*. Tello conceives of the
Church's outreach as quintessentially to the poor and the popular
social classes, the urban workers, *villistas* (people in the impoverished
villas de miseria), small town inhabitants, and *campesinos*. These constitute the majority of *concrete human persons* in Argentina, Latin
America, and indeed the whole world.

In the case of Latin America, something quite special occurred
in its initial evangelization five hundred years ago. A distinctive,
hybrid Christian culture came about, and its essence is captured in the
category of *pueblo* (people). The Church's mission to evangelize and
the pastoral action that flows from such a mission require paying
attention to this unique, popular culture made up of concrete human
persons that live in relationships, in family and communities that constitute a people. Consequently, the development of adequate popular
pastoral action in the spirit of Vatican II requires two things. On one
hand, the Church must find ways for the faithful, the people, to exercise leadership and ministry within it, and on the other the Church
must be engaged in the historic movement of the people that goes
beyond the Church itself. This involves uncovering the ways in which
the faithful people can become subjects of the Church's evangelizing

action and protagonists of the Gospel as well as objects or receivers of its activity.

TELLO AND BERGOGLIO

Juan Carlos Scannone summarizes the close correspondence between the salient features of Pope Francis's pontificate and key concepts of Tello's *La Teología del Pueblo.*[7] The apostolic exhortation *Evangelii gaudium* is basically a roadmap of where Francis aspires to lead the Church. To accomplish his Petrine ministry today, Pope Francis's leadership has taken the form of powerful symbolic gestures, personal and even electrifying interviews, and generally brief official and sometimes spontaneous, off-the-cuff remarks that communicate the message with words and phrases that grab people's attention and enhance the reception of his message in even the most hostile quarters of a skeptical, secularized world. The pope speaks of pastors who "smell of the sheep," God's "nearness and tenderness," a "culture of encounter," and a "maternal, inclusive" rather than a "judgmental, exclusive" Church. Scannone shows the affinity of the pope's remarkable reorientation of the Church, his fascinating gestalt, with the pastoral-theological vision of Rafael Tello. The beginnings of Tello's vision are found in his positive assessment of the people's religion that concurs completely with views found in episcopal documents from Medellín to Aparecida. The highest expression of this positive attitude toward popular religion is found in the *Concluding Document of Aparecida*, which refers to it as a "*mística popular.*"[8] *Evangelii gaudium* picks up this terminology and clearly states what the *mística popular* does: "The genius of each people receives in its own way the entire Gospel and embodies it in expressions of prayer, fraternity, justice, struggle and celebration" (no. 237).

Francis's teachings also correlate with the Theology of the People in several ways, for example, in the insistence on the importance of inculturation of the Gospel, the option for the most marginal, and transformative action in the promotion of justice. Both Pope Francis and Tello distance themselves from a pious religion of devotions that plays into an already problematic individualism and sentimentalism. Neither Francis nor Tello deny the need for the purification and maturation of popular religion (see *Evangelii gaudium* 68–70). Yet Francis and Tello insist that new, creative relationships between Christ and the people, Christ and the community, are forged within the crucible of popular religious devotion whose forms are incarnate:

> They entail a personal relationship, not with vague spiritual energies or powers but with God, with Mary, with the saints. These devotions are fleshy, they have a face. They are capable of fostering relationships and not just enabling escapism. (*Evangelii gaudium* 90)

Shortly after this affirmation in *Evangelii gaudium*, Pope Francis goes on to contrast the inherently communal thrust of popular Catholicism with an unacceptable "spirituality of well-being" divorced from community life. Likewise, he contrasts an authentic popular religion with a spirituality of prosperity that accepts little or no responsibility for the needs of the poor. There is no secret that he is referring to contemporary therapeutic trends in spirituality and to the "I'm-spiritual-but-not religious" mindset. Along the same lines, Pope Francis, in his talk to the bishops of CELAM in Brazil, insisted on the "creativity, healthy autonomy and liberty of the laity."[9] In the context of a critique of a clerical culture that sometimes inhibits the Church's evangelizing mission, he brought home a point about the people's religion as a form of Catholicism really lived by the people in a communitarian and adult way, and laudably manifesting itself in Latin America in the form of Bible study groups and base ecclesial communities.[10]

THE PEOPLE'S FAITH

An underlying conviction of both Tello's theology and the thinking of Pope Francis is found in both the *Concluding Document of Aparecida* and *Evangelii gaudium* in their affirmation of the role played by popular culture, the people, in the mission to evangelize. *Evangelii gaudium* states it clearly:

> We can see that the different peoples among whom the Gospel has been inculturated are active collective subjects

or agents of evangelization....Once the Gospel has been inculturated in a people, in their process of transmitting their culture they also transmit the faith in ever new forms....One can say that a people continuously evangelize itself. Here lies the importance of popular piety, a true expression of the spontaneous missionary activity of the people of God. This is an ongoing and developing process, of which the Holy Spirit is the principal agent. (no. 122)

Tello's theological work was focused on demonstrating the central role that popular Latin American culture has played in the ongoing evangelization of the continent. Being a confirmed Thomist, Tello develops the distinctions used by St. Thomas Aquinas in his analysis of the act of faith that builds on ideas first offered by St. Augustine and reflected upon by Peter Lombard. The classic statement of this nuanced way of thinking about faith is Aquinas's formulation, which states the following:

> Now it is one thing to say: "I believe in God" (*credere Deum*), for this indicates the object. It is another thing to say: "I believe God" (*credere Deo*), for this indicates the one who testifies. And it is still another thing to say: "I believe in God" (*credere in Deum*), for this indicates the end. Thus God can be regarded as the object of faith, as the one who testifies, and as the end, but in different ways. To believe in God (*in Deum*) as in an end is proper to faith living through the love of charity.[11]

Tello characterizes the way of faith of the popular social classes and the poor in terms of *credere in Deum*. He sees popular culture as particularly attuned to a loving trust in God, what perhaps might be called "systematic" belief, a trusting stance toward the world in which God is at the center that significantly contrasts with modernity's critical consciousness and tendency toward systematic doubt and exclusion of God. Tello does not dismiss the achievements of modernity, but he notes its limitations as well in that it gives pride of place to rationality and neglects or dismisses affectivity. Thus, the modern mindset distances itself from the simplicity of the gospel message that is captured in the precept to love God, oneself, and one's neighbor. As Thomas à Kempis observed long ago in *The Imitation of Christ*, "It is better to feel compunction than to know how to define it." Perhaps this is what Jesus was talking about in the Gospel when he insisted on the need to "become like children" in order to experience the reign of God (Matt 18:3). Both Tello and Bergoglio's teachings lead one to think that more needs to be said about the positive disposition of the poor toward God that is too often dismissed as simple naïvety by the "enlightened."

A description of the actual working of this disposition toward a loving trust in God in the case of the faithful people of God, the poor *campesinos* and the urban working class, is provided by Tello. He speaks of a *conocimiento afectivo* (affective knowledge). He takes this notion from St. Thomas Aquinas:

> It can be said that for St. Thomas there are two ways to assent to truth, two types of knowledge. One is speculative knowledge and the other is affective knowledge. St. Thomas presents affective knowledge as knowledge that properly pertains to the gift of wisdom. In order to practice wisdom the wise person must exercise judgment. That judgment takes two forms corresponding to two forms of wisdom. One is the wisdom that results in judgments based on reason derived from study. (In this sense, speculative theology is wisdom.) There is, however, another form of wisdom that a wise person possesses as a result of his or her affective tendencies and moral and religious habits which put that person in contact with whatever it is about which one exercises judgment.[12]

For Tello, popular culture provides a locus for the gestation of a truly inculturated faith that requires the kind of loving trust in God and wisdom that comes with "affective knowledge." Pope Francis considers popular piety the most salient expression of popular culture in the Latin American context and also a great source of wisdom. In *Evangelii gaudium*, he devotes a section of his apostolic exhortation to what he calls "the evangelizing power of popular piety" (nos. 122–26). In this section, the pope cites the same references to St. Thomas

Aquinas's *Summa Theologiae* used by Tello in which the distinction is made between *credere Deum* and *credere in Deum*:

> The Aparecida Document describes the riches which the Holy Spirit pours forth in popular piety by his gratuitous initiative. On that beloved continent, where many Christians express their faith through popular piety, the bishops also refer to it as "popular spirituality" or "the people's mysticism." It is truly a spirituality incarnated in the culture of the lowly. Nor is it devoid of content; rather it discovers and expresses that content more by way of symbols than by discursive reasoning, and in the act of faith greater accent is placed on *credere in Deum* than on *credere Deum*.

By saying that the faith of the poor is more precisely grasped by St. Thomas's distinction about various forms of faith, Tello and Pope Francis point to the affective nature of the knowledge of the poor, which is more closely associated with *credere in Deum*, faith that becomes life through love, rather than through mere intellectual ascent.

There are many other distinctive teachings of Rafael Tello that correlate well with the pastoral vision of Pope Francis. Fundamentally, Tello, even more than Lucio Gera, was focused on the development of what he insistently called *pastoral popular*, that is, pastoral care and outreach that respects the distinctive qualities of popular culture and its role as the locus for gestating or incubating the faith. This is a central concern of *La Teología del Pueblo*, which makes important distinctions between (1) modern Enlightenment culture, (2) ecclesiastical culture, and (3) popular culture. Pope Francis's persistent concern with "spiritual worldliness" reflects his recognition of certain tendencies of ecclesiastical culture toward corruption and even heresy, for example, neopelagianism and gnosticism. The pope discusses this in *Evangelii gaudium* and identifies pharisaical, neopelagian, and gnostic tendencies among church leaders as a particularly harmful proclivity (see nos. 94–96). The gnostic tendency shows itself in an exaggerated tendency to focus one's attention on certain ideas and experiences, to become subjective and self-absorbed in one's thoughts and pet notions rather than attentive to reality. A neopelagian tendency shows itself in a self-induced sense of one's own superiority over others due to one's ability to live up to certain norms. This, in turn, can lead to the self-reference and narcissism frequently denounced by Pope Francis.

The choice of Pope Francis to communicate through gesture, symbol, and narrative more than in a discursive theological manner and to even cite teachings of his grandmother and of the ordinary faithful in his preaching point to a preference for popular culture as an indispensable vehicle for effective evangelization in many ordinary contexts. Both Enlightenment and ecclesiastical cultures, with their tendency toward rationalism and abstraction, are somewhat shunned by Pope Francis. In *La Iglesia al Servicio del Pueblo*, Tello helps one understand the pope's stance by describing how popular culture approaches the mystery of faith:

> In the case of our people faith is lived as a simple handing over, a commitment, more than as rational knowledge of truths. Hence what predominates in this act is *affective theology* which develops a popular wisdom that sees God present in life and knows him as a result of his provident presence. In popular Christianity faith is the conviction that God is not alien to life itself and engages in it, and that God can actually be found in the profound experiences that fill our lives.[13]

The most important point to make about Tello's drive toward the development of a *pastoral popular* is that the Church's commitment to its mission to evangelize rises and falls precisely on popular culture's ability to provide ways for real inculturation of the faith in people's lives. In Europe and the rest of the so-called First World, and in most ecclesiastical circles, there is a tendency toward self-reference that leads the Church to often take the road of pragmatic or technical rationality and speculative theology in its approach to bridging the gap between faith and culture rather than that of an affective theology that arises *desde*, that is, "*from*" the people. This affective way is the way of popular culture as Tello articulated in his many talks and until now unpublished writings—a labor of love that, nevertheless, had a profound effect on the thinking of Argentine theological circles in which Jorge Bergoglio moved all his life.

For those who speak Spanish, what is being pointed out here is particularly pertinent for the *campesinos* and urban working class. The use of the term *Diosito* to refer to God exemplifies the difference between "enlightened," ecclesiastical culture's way and that of popular culture. The use of the Spanish diminutive *ito* in reference to the deity is, of course, not about God's size, but rather about one's affective disposition toward persons. God is subjectively viewed as lovable and supremely approachable by the person using this term. This love allows the person to know God in a way that goes beyond intellectual knowledge alone. This way of talking implies intimacy with God that somehow the poor seem to attain and express. This reality points in turn to the indispensable role that the people or popular culture can and must play in the evangelization of cultures through the inculturation of faith.

In a substantial article written by Cardinal Bergoglio after his positive experience at the 2007 Aparecida Conference, he lays out a coherent vision of evangelization that gives pride of place to a theological anthropology that shuns imposition of Church teaching and superficial, moralistic, or rationalist adaptations to culture. He insists that the Church's mission must take seriously the particularity and historical context of each culture, fidelity to the apostolic tradition, and fidelity to the worldwide ecclesial communion.[14] In doing so, however, the Church must put the emphasis on God's mercy, tenderness, and nearness, and not on the clarity of dogmas and theological propositions about God. Such a pastoral strategy will contribute to winning over people's hearts and lead to what Bernard Lonergan called "affective conversion."[15]

More needs to be said about Tello's understanding of the three prevailing cultural contexts for evangelization already alluded to in regard to bringing about affective conversion to the gospel: (1) the culture of the Enlightenment or modernity, (2) ecclesiastical culture, and (3) popular culture. With regard to modernity, Tello insists that it is intrinsically antievangelical even though it is certainly not bereft of positive values. Its main defect has to do with its view of life that brackets transcendence and falls into immanentism. This is the problem of secularism. Moreover, modernity tends to move people toward individualism, away from any sense of solidarity, and in the direction of consumerism and materialism. Christianity proposes something quite different, especially from modernity's structural discrimination and disdain for the poor. It is not that persons in modern cultures are totally unable to assimilate gospel values, but rather that their culture is notably averse to the transmission of Christ's core message. The Church, consequently, must become ever more aware of the modern world's challenges to the gospel and find constructive ways to respond to them.

The second cultural context—surprisingly for some—that does not advance the evangelization of people in Latin America, and one might infer beyond, is ecclesiastical culture. At first, it appears quite adequate in view of its seeming compatibility with the gospel and link to long-standing traditions. The problem with ecclesiastical culture, according to Tello, is that it does not reach the majority of Latin Americans because it is not within the peculiar historical current of the earlier evangelization of the sixteenth and seventeenth centuries. This is the period of gestation that created a "Christian people" in Latin America and not "ecclesial communities." What he is referring to is the fact that the faith was first taught in Latin America as something to be lived within the context of a people (the wider culture) and not so much in the context of ecclesial institutions. Hence, the adhesion of Latin American Catholics to the parish and other institutions seems relatively tenuous in comparison to that of U.S. Catholics, while the notion of institutional stewardship remains rather undeveloped as well. They are quite loyal in contrast to *popular* associations and the wider culture linked to the Church but not directly under ecclesiastical control. A further issue affecting the process of evangelization in and through ecclesiastical culture is the fact that it has been compromised and tainted by modernity, imbued with elements of individualism and narcissism. Church culture can put too much emphasis on individual effort and personal sin, overestimate the role of pragmatic reason in people's lives, and not prioritize human interdependence and solidarity. An ecclesial culture tainted with these qualities of modernity is a turn-off for a major part of the Latin American masses, especially the poor, if not for the worldwide, popular masses in general. The popular social classes are more fixed on the need of salvation understood as liberation from all kinds of oppression. Ecclesiastical culture refers to the formation of communities of faith that are institutionalized in structures like the parish, the diocese, and even in the Petrine ministry, as the papacy is called. Manifestations of this culture or subculture are found in external trappings, hierarchical distinctions, protocols, *cursus honoris*, and other expressions that have arisen over time in the conduct of the Church's daily life. Popular culture keeps its distance from much of this, not because it necessarily finds official church culture disagreeable or opposes it, but because the concerns of church culture are often rather distant, irrelevant, or outside the realm of interest or possibility to the popular social classes.

Tello provides a rich and contrasting description of popular Latin American culture. He maintains that it constitutes what the bishops at Puebla called a new cultural way of living the Christian faith, an *originalidad histórica cultural*, a historical cultural originality or novelty. This new way of living the faith shows itself in its ability to respond to a vast range of life situations with true gospel values. Bianchi adds this to the description:

> This culture or way of grounding oneself in the face of life and death finds its roots in Christian faith. It expresses itself above all in the desire to acknowledge human dignity and in an existential attitude that recognizes God's presence in everyday life and in the eternal destiny of that life.[16]

Tello insists that it is precisely attention to popular culture that will contribute to the realization of a fruitful way for pursuing "pastoral conversion" and furthering the new evangelization. In the following chapter, some important threads of Pope Francis's emergent pastoral vision will be explored. These threads resonate with much of the original insights and concerns of Rafael Tello highlighted here.

Chapter Five

EVANGELIZATION, SPIRITUALITY, AND JUSTICE

One of the more helpful resources for deeper analysis of the sociocultural and spiritual aspects of Pope Francis's theological vision is found in the seminal thought of the Brazilian Jesuit missiologist and anthropologist Marcello Azevedo (1927–2010). Azevedo was a prolific writer and teacher, a theological pioneer, who wrote on the Church's understanding of its identity and mission in the modern world as taught by the Second Vatican Council. He also wrote extensively on spirituality out of the Ignatian heritage. Like Jorge Mario Bergoglio, Azevedo lived through the exciting decades of renewal that Latin America experienced in the wake of the Council. He specialized in the study of anthropological concept of culture as found in *Gaudium et spes* and its relevance to the Church's missionary identity. He realized that the age of fortress Church was over and that the early decades of the third millennium, even more than the last fifty years of the second millennium, would be a time of epochal change for the Church.

Three interrelated currents of thought particularly relevant to the understanding of Pope Francis were the focus of much of Azevedo's thought: (1) evangelization of culture, (2) transformative action on behalf of justice or liberation, and (3) Christian spirituality appropriate for the new epoch. Even though Azevedo did not live to see the reforms of Pope Francis, a study of Azevedo's writings reveals that he foresaw some of the change in tone and new direction that the Argentine pope would later bring to the worldwide Church. This chapter considers some of the important features of Pope Francis's distinctive vision of a Church for the third millennium as illuminated by Azevedo's seminal ideas.[1]

THE CHURCH CONFRONTS MODERNITY

One of Azevedo's studies provides a strong rationale for the reforms initiated by Pope Francis. *Vivir la Fe en un Mundo Plural: Discrepancias y Convergencias* (Living the Faith in a Pluralistic World: Discrepancies and Convergences) is the mature fruit of Azevedo's research, teaching, and writing over several decades.[2] His thesis does not contradict Tello's and Gera's critical reading of modern culture. Azevedo would agree with their analysis regarding the tension between modern culture and the gospel, particularly in relation to the popular social classes. Nevertheless, like Pope Francis, Azevedo maintains that the response to this tension cannot be the dismissal of the modern world nor a retreat into tradition and a narrow circumscribed identity, but rather engagement. Azevedo focuses on the Church's critical engagement with modern and postmodern culture. As such, Azevedo's thought complements that of Tello's and Gera's *La Teología del Pueblo*.

The Brazilian Jesuit begins by pointing out that the context for the Church's pursuit of its evangelizing mission in today's world has drastically changed. As a result, there must be a change in thinking among church leaders and the faithful themselves. That change requires that the culture of modernity be approached with openness rather than suspicion because no culture should be dismissed or deemed impermeable to gospel values. In other words, just as the Church seeks to engage diversity in the form of nationality, ethnicity, and social class with the truths of the gospel as it has throughout history, so too must it engage the paradigmatic culture of modernity and postmodernity today with its tendencies toward individualism, consumerism, and secularism. No culture is without values and possibilities for growth or totally impervious to change. There is a difference between a critical assessment of modernity that keeps the doors of dialogue open while remaining in continuity with the received tradition on the one hand and a reactionary stance that retreats into the certainties of the past and falls into a deadening traditionalism on the other. This latter stance relates to the modern world in a hostile, dismissive way, with negativity, suspicion, and fear. This response is not appropriate in light of the gospel and ecclesial practice over the ages, a missionary practice that accounts for the global reach of Catholicism and demonstrates its ability to engage each and every culture without discounting any of them.

God's love and mercy as revealed in the Gospels is for all people, cultures, and times. Thus, God's love and the message of salvation are universal and relevant even to the culture of modernity. Indeed, the Church has often learned something and gained insights into the human reality and God from cultures deemed antagonistic to Christianity, for example, the pagan cultures of Greece and Rome. Azevedo's approach reflects the insights of the Second Vatican Council, particularly *Gaudium et spes* with its great optimism toward the modern world and *Nostra aetate* on interreligious dialogue with its acknowledgment of the Holy Spirit's presence in other religions besides Christianity. The new optimism regarding the relationship between faith and contemporary culture championed by the Second Vatican Council did, however, bring with it many tensions, and they are still very much with the Church. What is new is that in the age of Pope Francis, those tensions have been candidly acknowledged and put on the table for discussion as never before. Rather than closing off dialogue, Pope Francis insists on it as the fundamental condition for carrying out the Church's evangelizing mission.

THE RELATIONSHIP BETWEEN THE CHURCH AND THE WORLD

Tension between the Church and the world has, of course, always existed. That tension was exacerbated at the time of the Protestant Reformation and over the last five hundred years as the social and cultural order forged over the first millennium gradually eroded. The Church confronted and attempted to address the issue in various forms and at crucial moments in history, notably at the time of the Catholic Reformation in the sixteenth and seventeenth centuries, after the shock of the French Revolution, and more directly toward the end of the nineteenth century and the early years of the twentieth. Authoritative responses to the challenges of the emerging modern world in this long period tended to be negative and widened the gap between the Church and the modern world. The modernist controversy that produced Pius IX's *Syllabus of Errors*, St. Pius X's *Oath Against Modernism*, and the conflict of the Vatican with the American bishops over what was called Americanism exemplify how the Church at the highest levels resisted serious dialogue with the culture of modernity.

Yet there were seeds of dialogue to be found in the influential writings of European theologians of the first half of the twentieth century and in the theological movements called *ressourcement* and the *nouvelle theologie*, whose concerns and products laid the foundations of the Second Vatican Council. Among those associated with these developments—to name just a few—are the Jesuits: Henri de Lubac, Jean Danielou, Karl Rahner, and John Courtney Murray; the Dominicans: Marie-Dominique Chenu, Ives Congar, and Edward Schillebeeckx, and diocesan priests: Hans Kung, Joseph Ratzinger (later Pope Benedict XVI), and Pietro Pavan.

The Second Vatican Council clearly made progress in moving away from the fortress church mentality, yet, for a period of more than thirty years under Popes John Paul II and Benedict XVI, there were strong, influential elements of the Church in the Roman Curia and among national bishops' conferences throughout the world but especially in Italy, Spain, the United States, and Latin America, who pushed more in the direction of resistance to modernity rather than dialogue with it. They manifested a preference for an antagonistic "culture war" stance for the Church toward the world around it. Some ecclesial movements rallied around the preservation of the Latin Mass and others, like the Legionnaires of Christ and even Opus Dei, which originally functioned as a new model of apostolic engagement adapted to the circumstances of the modern world, emerged as instruments of a more guarded attitude toward that world and came to be identified with a Christendom mentality, that is, the Church as privileged overseer of culture rather than as a collaborator in its development. It should be added, however, that the public perception of the tension within the Church regarding how to relate to the modern world and the characterizations of some of these movements have been unduly influenced by the mass media, which unfortunately prefers sound-bites to nuanced reporting. Conflictive and antagonistic interpretations produce polarization. The result is often more a caricature than an accurate representation of the facts.[3]

POPE BENEDICT XVI AND THE CHURCH'S ENCOUNTER WITH MODERNITY

Pope Benedict XVI did at times contribute to the perception that the Church was drifting back toward a Christendom mentality with his role as doctrinal watchdog, encouragement of the Latin liturgy, and support for the "reform of the reform" movement's traditionalist leanings. He made many efforts to reach out to traditionalist groups like the followers of the schismatic Archbishop Marcel Lefebvre. Nevertheless, in all fairness, it must be said that he did manifest a keen understanding of the nature of the tension between Christian faith and modernity and explicitly referred to this tension in his first Christmas address to the Roman Curia in 2005. He was concerned with the question of how to properly interpret the Second Vatican Council, specifically in relation to the need of the Church to engage the modern world. Pope Benedict XVI's substantive description of the situation seems particularly apt in view of Pope Francis's renewed call for dialogue with the modern world, an invitation that necessarily raises questions about how to appropriately interpret the authoritative stance of the Second Vatican Council on this matter. Pope Benedict XVI reflects on the crucial question of how to interpret Vatican II:

> On the one hand, there is an interpretation that I would call "a hermeneutic of discontinuity and rupture"; it has frequently availed itself of the sympathies of the mass media, and also one trend of modern theology. On the other, there is the "hermeneutic of reform," of renewal in the continuity of the one subject-Church which the Lord has given to us. She is a subject which increases in time and develops, yet always remains the same, the one subject of the journeying People of God.[4]

Pope Benedict XVI continues in this address with a perceptive analysis of the nature of the tension between the Church and the modern world in terms of three neuralgic points: (1) the relationship between faith and modern science, both natural and historical; (2) the relationship between the Church and the modern State, a relationship that gives room for diversity of religion and ideologies; and (3) the relationship between Christian faith and world religions themselves. In what sounds like a reflection quite relevant to the "pastoral conversion" requested of Pope Francis, one that seeks to engage new realities while being faithful to Church teaching, Pope Benedict XVI observes,

> It is precisely in this combination of continuity and discontinuity at different levels that the very nature of true reform consists. In this process of innovation in continuity we must learn to understand *more practically than before* that the Church's decisions are contingent matters—for example, certain practical forms of liberalism or a free interpretation of the Bible—should necessarily be contingent themselves, precisely because they refer to specific reality that is changeable in itself. It was necessary to learn to recognize that in these decisions it is only the principles that express the permanent aspect, since they remain as an undercurrent, motivating decisions from within. On the other hand, not so permanent are practical forms that depend on the historical situation and are therefore subject to change.[5]

AZEVEDO ON THE CHURCH'S RESPONSE TO THE CHALLENGES OF MODERNITY

Marcello Azevedo describes the nature of the tension between the Church and the world in another way that is not necessarily contradictory to that of Pope Benedict XVI. Azevedo highlights the centuries-old tendency of the Church to see itself as the principle arbiter of culture, a role it had played for centuries, at least in the Western world.[6] *Gaudium et spes*, however, ushered in a new era in which the

Church finally admitted that it cannot and ought not serve as the principle arbiter of a wide-ranging Christian/Catholic culture, a role the Roman Catholic Church assumed since the time of Constantine. Some have called this approach the Christendom model, a potent, top-down fusion of Christian concepts with the prevailing power elites that flourished under the union of church and state. With the Second Vatican Council, the Church began to admit that the Constantinian or Christendom mentality was out-of-date and exhausted. The Church at Vatican II did an about-face and disavowed its longstanding teaching regarding the ideal of church-state union and endorsed the modern concept of separation of church and state.[7] Yet many elements of the Church including some bishops and other influential leaders and thinkers lagged behind. They appeared to be stuck with the residue of the older mentality, perhaps sometimes out of nostalgia and a lack of imagination, or at other times out of a laudable but misguided regard for ecclesial tradition and continuity with the past.

Nevertheless, Pope Benedict XVI attempted to dispel some of the conflict between Catholicism and the modern world in his 2008 visit to France. He pointed out the fundamental role of Christianity in the West, particularly through the instrument of monasticism, in the establishment of principles of human dignity and regard for reason and scientific inquiry upon which the modern world and the autonomy of the secular are built.[8] He reiterated his insistence on the importance of dialogue with all cultures including the modern secular culture in his promotion of the "Courtyard of the Gentiles" initiative in 2011. The pope critiqued the assumption that there is an inherent conflict between modernity and Christianity by showing how modernity is in point of fact historically unthinkable without the foundations provided it in the Christian culture of the West.[9] Bedrock Christian principles of human dignity and rights, including those of women, and regard for intelligence and scientific inquiry of all kinds played an essential role in the rise of the modern spirit over centuries.[10]

Yet Pope Benedict XVI's obvious predilection for solemn and formal liturgy, even one in Latin, gave a mixed message. More significantly, the persistent investigation and silencing of theological voices on the part of the Vatican's Doctrinal Congregation in the period after Vatican II contributed to a climate of cognitive dissonance, fear, and theological disengagement from critical issues. Some elements in the Church, notably some seminarians and young priests, gave the impression that the Church must become a remnant and retreat behind its ancient rituals and symbols like a sect in a hostile world. Pope Benedict XVI's authorization of the Extraordinary Rite in Latin fed into this attitude that at times seemed to be in conflict with the theological vision of *Gaudium et spes* and *Sacrosanctum concilium*. It was no secret that Argentine enthusiasts of the Latin liturgy did not look kindly upon Cardinal Bergoglio, who did not share their conviction that promoting the Latin liturgy is a top priority.[11] They think even less of him as Bishop of Rome! He certainly does not promote the Latin liturgy, especially the Tridentine version of it, as a way to effectively reach out to today's youth or anyone else except to a rather limited circle of true believers.

FROM UNIFORMITY TO DIVERSITY

The Latin Mass enthusiasts are, of course, only part of a greater rearguard movement within the Church over the past fifty years. On the part of a rising number of ecclesial voices in the period after Vatican II, a less engaging and more defensive posture was proposed for the Church, one that froze or prolonged the centuries-long response of the Church to the Protestant Reformation and to the disasters that ensued in the wake of the French Revolution. After the initial excitement about reform and renewal proposed by the Second Vatican Council, significant elements of church leadership, never a majority, fell back into a longstanding, defensive posture with regard to the modern world and encouraged a response to the challenges of modernity that emphasized orthodoxy, the preservation of custom, the return to the use of Latin in the liturgy, and the restoration of certain protocols and usages from the past five centuries. This fortress mentality gave rise to an argumentative and intellectualizing stance that emphasized apologetics and what is sometimes called the new apologetics. Accordingly, rules, legalities, and moral strictures particularly regarding matters relating to sexuality and bioethics received the lion's share of attention.

In contrast, Azevedo formulated principles for a dynamic, expansive response to the challenges of modernity, one different from what he called the "culturalist" approach of traditionalists. The Church's outreach in today's world accordingly must integrate inculturation with liberation and with an authentic spirituality. This stance involves not only *giving* or sharing values with the cultures that the Church encounters on its way in history, but also *receiving* from them. This engagement has a powerful *prospective* dimension to it rather than an almost entirely *retrospective* attitude. Pope Francis almost always refers to evangelization of culture *and* inculturation of the faith together, and encourages proclamation of the good news through dialogue with others and witness in a totally invitational rather than imposing manner. This give-and-take is absolutely fundamental to inculturation. In order to receive, one must maintain a stance of openness toward one's conversation or dialogue partner. Consequently, the notion that the Church has *all* the truth about God and other matters of ultimate concern, an attitude that Catholic fundamentalists seem to harbor, is profoundly antithetical to the Church's evangelizing mission. In *Lumen gentium*, the Council Fathers established a principle that continues to guide the Church today, especially in the age of Pope Francis, one that contributes to an attitude of true missionary engagement. The principle is clear: "Many elements of sanctification and of truth are found outside its [the Church's] visible confines" (*Lumen gentium* 8).

Similarly, it must be acknowledged that evangelization as inculturation also includes transformative action for justice or what Pope John Paul II often called liberation. Here, Azevedo captures the nature of the challenge and clarifies how such a process and emphasis on transformative action on behalf of justice can successfully unfold and provide an antidote to the hunkering down mentality of "culture warriors":

> The integration of inculturation and liberation in an experiential and critical perspective, principally in the contexts of injustice and suffering of Third World nations, offers an alternative to the "culturalist" approach which centers itself on culture as a source of isolation and tends to disassociate culture from society. Consequently the theological

and missiological focus is placed on the intended evangelization of the culture *from outside in*, a patent or discreet form of domination without a consistent inculturation of the Gospel and without the required attention to the context of real society in which one lives or will live.[12]

EVANGELIZING FROM THE INSIDE OUT

The key concept here is the critique of evangelization from "outside in" rather than from "inside out." An approach to evangelization that conceives of culture in a static, univocal, one-shoe-fits-all way and proposes to convert culture from the "outside in," in a dominating manner, is inappropriate and ineffective. Such a one-sided, exclusivist approach also fails to integrate the Church's evangelizing activity (inculturation) with spirituality and with transformative social action. Such an approach is the source of what Azevedo calls a serious disconnect between faith and life. This, in turn, leads to the scarcity of or even growing absence of individual or collective ethical expressions in cultures, and to an evangelization that, as Pope Paul VI describes it in *Evangelii nuntiandi*, is superficial like painting a coat of varnish on the outside (see no. 20). This leads to experiencing faith as something publically professed and even affirmed in the rituals of civic religion and ritually incorporated into institutions, but hardly practiced in day-to-day life. A disconnect between faith and life was already obvious to the Latin American bishops in the years immediately after the Second Vatican Council. This dualism was seen in Latin America in the often arbitrary and unjust conduct of governments and other institutions on the one hand and the fervent religiosity of the populace on the other. Something similar is seen in the United States in the relative popularity of religions, the many expressions of faith in God heard in civic discourse, along with an ever-growing materialism, consumerism, and a drift toward religious superficiality exemplified among the youth. According to sociologist Christian Smith, significant numbers of American teenagers, for example, practice a "moralistic therapeutic deism" that more or less trivializes religion.[13]

In response to the need for an authentic inculturation of the faith, Azevedo describes how true integration of faith and life must occur. The central question here revolves around the degree to which the Church is prepared to reach out to the modern world, the extent to which it is willing to engage this world and on what terms. Azevedo points out that over the past five hundred years in the post-Tridentine era up until the Second Vatican Council and even beyond it, the Church's response emphasized the need to assure *uniformity* if the Church were to remain united. Uniformity was everything in doctrine, liturgical practice, pastoral care, and catechesis. In the United States, despite the strong libertarian current in its culture, this drive toward uniformity was actually exacerbated by a corresponding drive toward standardization facilitated by the print medium and other forms of modern communications. The European American Catholic Church in the United States from its East Coast origins (in contrast to the Hispanic Church) has been a fine example of a Tridentine Church, that is, one that tries and often succeeds in following the standardizations required by that reform-minded Council.[14]

What perhaps has yet to be accepted and appreciated is that Vatican II represents a break with this Tridentine drive toward uniformity and standardization in at least some respects. The Council's insistence on openness to cultures and dialogue as a *sine qua non* for the Church in pursuit of its contemporary mission requires another mentality. The role of uniformity so prized in the defensive, post-Tridentine period of Church history gives way with Vatican II to respect for diversity, which, interestingly, is not a new emphasis, but rather one that picks up again and reinforces the Church's ancient catholicity, the pursuit of communion in difference rather than communion in sameness. Such a development moves the Church away from a univocal and dialectical mindset and imagination that see contradictions and conflicts everywhere and want to constantly "draw lines in the sand." What is needed now more than ever is an inclusive, analogical mindset and imagination that discovers both commonalities and differences that enrich relationships rather than threaten them. *Inculturation* is the word used to signify the way in which such communion may be achieved. One need only reflect on Paul the Apostle's missionary journeys and the early controversies about circumcision and other Jewish customs to realize that inculturation or evangelization of culture has been a fundamental feature of the Church's life from its very origins.

The Protestant Reformation, however, moved the Church in the West away from its millennial practice of *lex orandi, lex credendi*, a principle closely linked to inculturation. This principle appreciated that faith is largely expressed and even formulated by the community *in practice* rather than by the hierarchy *in theory*, in a somewhat inductive rather than deductive manner, as well as in a symbolic and ritual way rather than a rationalistic and propositional one. For centuries, faith and life came together as it has to, in an open-ended way more by means of performance and narrative than by rational theological discourse or bureaucratic enforcement. The symbols and rituals of the Church's official worship and popular devotions served as vehicles of belief rather than the cold formulations of theological discourse. The Reformation, the rise of the print medium, and later, the Enlightenment coalesced to create a dialectical, either/or ethos within Western Christianity and the Western world. This ethos and preference for an either/or imagination tended to be driven by an inordinate need to clarify ambiguities in matters of doctrine and morality, to censure and excommunicate, thus promoting exclusion more than inclusion. Such a stance is toxic for the Church's catholicity. This, in turn, played into the rationalism of Enlightenment culture as well as of ecclesiastical culture with its neo-Scholastic philosophy, both of which tended to highlight black and white distinctions and sharp doctrinal divisions rather than commonalities. Finally, a tendency toward fundamentalism abetted by growing literacy and print culture infected both the Catholic and Protestant Churches from the sixteenth century onward, a tendency that affected not only traditionalists and those hankering for the certainties of the past, but also progressives who formulated their own increasingly rigid and nonnegotiable ideological boundaries.

The pursuit of ecclesial communion in diversity or difference rather than in uniformity of ideas and practices demands a deeper understanding of the relationship between faith and culture, one that grasps the *dynamic* character of this relationship and the inescapable need for ongoing dialogue between the Gospel proclamation and cultures including the culture of secular modernity. The Church must especially attend to the actual reception of the Christian message by the people in the context of their many cultures and recognize that it is never enough to communicate with "clear and distinct ideas" and sound doctrines without also attending to whether that teaching is really getting across, being received. If it is not, the cause may be in the communicator as much as it is in the receiver. The failure to effectively communicate, interestingly, may be more in the tone or demeanor of the communicator than in the actual content of the message. Anthropologist Edward Hall explains this in his seminal work *Beyond Cultures*. Pope Francis is definitely what Hall would call a "high context communicator." Francis emphasizes not only the content—the "what" of his communication—but most especially the "how" of it—gestures, affectivity, humor, and expressivity. For many cultures all over the world—particularly in the Southern Hemisphere—this is the way to effectively communicate.[15]

These rather far-reaching reflections inspired by Marcello Azevedo's writings may shed light on Pope Francis's project of Gospel-centered reform. They suggest that the Church under the Argentine pope is dramatically intensifying the Second Vatican Council's call for a new relationship with the modern world. At stake is an unfolding and expansion of the Church's catholicity. In an amazingly brief period of time, the "Francis Effect" is opening the Church and the world to new possibilities and relationships for the third millennium. A constitutive element of the Church's encounter with the modern world, however, also includes the pursuit of justice, the transformative action to liberate the poor and most vulnerable from everything that oppresses them.

JUSTICE FLOWS FROM FAITH

Pope Francis is facilitating a historic openness to diversity and change, at least in mood, for the entire Church. This development closely correlates to the Church's catholicity, a mark of the Church with foundations in the central teaching of Christianity itself, namely the incarnation: "For God so loved the world that he gave his only Son" (John 3:16). Faith in Jesus Christ is essentially marked by the incarnation of the Word in Jesus of Nazareth and in the personal encounter of believers with him. By faith, a relationship of acceptance of God's unconditional, universal love is established between God and humanity. But a prior condition is placed on one's *effective* reception of that love, namely *you have to share it with others*. What this means is that communion with God does not take place without a prior communion among human beings. One is reminded of St. John the Evangelist's assertion that "Those who say, 'I love God,' and hate their brothers or sisters, are liars" (1 John 4:20). Azevedo insists that this simple truth about the connection between love of God and love of neighbor has profound implications and grounds the close link between faith and justice:

> Sin manifests itself in us above all in the manifold forms of injustice which destroy the possibility or the quality of our relationship of love and truth with our neighbor. Thus it is urgent that justice be re-established, properly understood both in the biblical sense as righteousness and coherence of existential truth in us as well as in the social sense as respect for human rights and for the basic needs of persons and communities....Because the relationship between faith and life, between faith and the totality of the human person's material and spiritual existence, between faith and the construction of a just society, is inherent to Christian faith and to the Gospel project.[16]

Rooting Christian life in the mystery of God's love as exemplified in the incarnation of the Word is fundamental for showing how faith and justice relate to each other. The pursuit of justice for a person of faith is not primarily a matter of ethics or morality. Rather, it is about experiencing the communion of love between and among God and oneself and one's neighbor. "Neighbor," of course, is understood as Jesus illustrates it in the parable of the Good Samaritan: one's neighbor is the one who is "different," the person one is not close to or from whom one is even estranged! This also means that the fullness of human salvation-liberation does not consist in merely constructing a more just, participative society of solidarity. Such a world, after all, could be built around nonevangelical values. The point for the Christian is that the Gospel proposes that such a world is constituted precisely in the connection between faith and justice by the overflow of one's love of God manifested in love of neighbor, in one's transformative action in the world of social, economic, political, cultural, and ecological concerns.

An evangelical take on justice includes an integral transformation of one's interpersonal relationships as well as
those with nature that ultimately reach fulfilment in one's
relationship with God....The service of faith and promotion of justice therefore presuppose a total reordering of
the human person's and society's presence in history; they
bring with them a radical reorientation of one's action in
the world and on it. It is only as a result of the coherence
between this dynamic of communion among ourselves
that the road is opened for the possibility of our communion with God.[17]

The integration of faith and life that results in action to promote
justice in the world is a natural and necessary consequence of taking the
truth of the incarnation seriously. Pope Francis calls this *Samaritanidad*
(Samaritanness). While not necessarily adding a great deal to the content—to the core convictions of Catholic social teaching—Pope
Francis's remarks and insistence on matters of social concern like immi-
gration, economic inequality, and the ecology do not come across as
moralistic. These concerns seem to find their source in a profoundly
faithful and spiritual vision that flows from the whole person rather
than just the intelligence or predictable ideologies of the left or the
right. That is why Pope Francis's teachings and actions for the promotion of justice possess an urgency and freshness about them that draws
people's attention and add an element of spark.

THE OPTION FOR THE POOR

Within the framework of this conversation about how faith
becomes life through the Church's efforts to evangelize cultures and
promote salvation-liberation in Christ, Azevedo, like Pope Francis,
raises the issue of the preferential, but not exclusive, option for the poor.
The central point that this option seeks to make in and for the
Church is that the most concrete and compelling way in which the
incarnational love of God for all humanity is demonstrated and
humanity's love for its fellow human beings manifested is through
concern for and attention to the socioeconomically poor, and not just
to the unborn. Charity, advocacy, and empowerment that promote

the life of the most vulnerable give witness in the most compelling, attractive way to the love of God and neighbor as understood in the Gospels. Hence, the option for the poor is essential to the Church's evangelizing mission in the world. Through this ongoing "mindfulness of the poor," to use St. Luke's phrase from the Acts of the Apostles, the Church concretizes for every age the truth and authenticity of its faith in Jesus Christ. Care of the poor is the single most obvious, quintessential way in which Christians demonstrate that faith and life in a Christian framework go together.

Concern for the poor, however, cannot be limited to simple acts of charity, even though this activity is laudable. The option for the poor must include advocacy and empowerment if it is not to revert to "assistencialism," mere band aids rather than remedies. The Church insists that not only the consequences of injustice and poverty be addressed but also their roots and systemic underpinnings in social, economic, and political structures. The *Catechism of the Catholic Church* and Catholic social teaching refer to this as "structural sin" (no. 1869).[18] The reality of structural sin embedded in social and economic systems was highlighted in the two Synods on Marriage and the Family, especially in the survey that went out after the first session. For example, in the section of the survey concerned with caring for wounded families, the question asked is, "How does the Christian community engage in alleviating the social and economic factors which often determine this situation?"[19] One of the great challenges facing the Church—and Pope Francis has spoken much about it—is the prevalence of socially unjust structures and the "globalization of indifference" with respect to the resolution of so many injustices. Despite some hopeful economic developments in China, Southeast Asia, and parts of Latin America, neither free-market capitalist nor collectivist ideologies have yet to offer satisfactory solutions to the challenge of poverty and growing inequality in the world. The Synod of Bishops' 1971 document titled *Justice in the World* already stated that the pursuit of justice is a constitutive element of the Church's mission. This means that evangelization includes liberation in all its forms—personal and social, material and spiritual. Like Pope Francis, however, Azevedo takes a clearly nuanced position and cautions the would-be evangelizer about the significance of the Church's option for the poor in connection with the allure of ideology and partisanship:

There is such a profound evangelical basis for this option
that it ought to be able to purify, relativize or eliminate all
the ways that one gets ideologically distracted and lost
through self-absorption in a too simplistic identification
between the option for the poor and some partisan political platform.[20]

HOW TO ENGAGE THE WORLD TODAY

At the heart of Marcelo Azevedo's understanding of what the
Church's evangelizing mission means today is first of all the conviction that the engagement with secular culture is absolutely crucial.
The biggest problem with the defensive, cultural warrior approach
that some church leaders appeared to favor in the decades immediately following the Second Vatican Council is that it is based on an
erroneous premise, namely that there is something inherently bad
about secular culture that disqualifies much of it from consideration
as cultural context for preaching the Gospel and encountering Jesus
Christ. If they have demonstrated anything, the first years of Pope
Francis's papacy have exemplified that, in principle, secularized, modern culture does not always exclude God or totally eliminate the
human, religious sensibility. The pope's explicit reference to homosexuality in his famous interview on the plane flying back from Rio
de Janeiro in 2013 exemplified a creative, new way in which to engage
a complex issue near to the heart of secular culture without under-
mining gospel values. Rather, the pope evoked the Gospel—specifically the seventh chapter of Matthew's Gospel—quite vividly with his
use of the words "who am I to judge?"

Second, authentic evangelization begins with an explicit proclamation of the Gospel applied to life as it really is and not with a
refined theological rationalization about the faith. The implication is
that evangelization requires the evangelizer to start often not with his
or her premises but rather with those of the culture being addressed;
in this case, with the reality and the premises of secular culture. Pope
Francis's repeated reference to "reality being more important than
ideas" echoes this insight of Azevedo's, as does Papa Bergoglio's
description of the Church as a field hospital in a war zone. The
specter of secularism, the ostensible exclusion of God and religion

from life, should not make the evangelizer hesitate to engage secular culture and its values and concerns, for example, its relentless promotion of equality based on human dignity that was a primordial concern of the Christian Gospel before the modern world ever existed.

Third, the gospel message has to be communicated. As already noted, this is different from conveying mere information. The message needs to be attractive and actionable, that is, invite the participation of the hearer. There must be an interaction between the one who proclaims and the receiver of the proclamation. This interaction begins to take shape in the process by which the evangelizer establishes a relationship with others. To evangelize is not to transfer the content of faith from one brain to another. Rather, it is the communication of grace and life. The so-called "Francis Effect" has much to do with the ability of Pope Francis to communicate in terms of gesture and image. For example, the photograph of him washing the feet of women, including a Muslim woman, was probably a more effective way to communicate the gospel than an entire papal encyclical about interreligious dialogue. The over-all impression that many receive from Pope Francis is that he is truly engaged with others and with human existence. He speaks with authority in a way that reminds one of Matthew 7:29: "For he taught them as one having authority, and not as their scribes." Some have observed, for instance, that he seems to enjoy being pope! His demeanor exudes authority and witnesses to the integrity between the outward function of the successor of Peter, or the Petrine ministry as it is called, and the man of flesh and blood, Jorge Mario Bergoglio.

This authenticity is sometimes lacking in religious leaders who depend on the outward trappings more than on the interior disposition. Pope Francis witnesses to a human life as well as to a life of faith *lived with profundity* and gusto. For example, his revelations about his love of tango, of literature, poetry, and the opera all speak to his listeners as demonstrations of a sparkling humanity, a wholesomeness and coherence in life and action, and not just in ideas. The challenge to evangelization and to the evangelizer is how to demonstrate that this wholeness or holiness can actually be lived in secular society, in the world as it actually is. For centuries, it seems that many Catholics have popularly held the notion that one really cannot do that. They tended to believe that monks and nuns, men and women religious, and priests are somehow holier than the ordinary baptized person. Accordingly, the holy people are all in retreat from the big, bad world! Pope Francis seems to be calling such a mindset into question, bringing such a fearful mentality to an end by the shining example of his outgoing way of being with others, especially the suffering and marginal, even in such a high-profile position as pope.

Linked to the notion of evangelization as real, persuasive communication is the fundamental conviction that evangelization is not primarily the communication of an intellectual content, of knowledge, principles, and doctrines. It is not even about induction into a world of certain methods, rituals, practices, and ways of teaching, either individually or in community. Rather, evangelization is foremost an adventure and project all about ongoing *conversion and spiritual growth*, the transformation of individuals and communities from the inside out—living the human reality in depth. It is precisely this orientation toward human integration and depth that gives weight to the appealing gestures, images, and reforms of Pope Francis.

Of course, there has to be something to integrate. One must begin with one's humanity. Pope Francis puts those very human qualities out on display all the time. The appropriateness and winning qualities of this sometimes "folksy" humanity contrast with certain antithetical tendencies of so-called religious people to "spiritualize" and disembody. Ecclesiastical culture and "churchiness" can tend toward a deadening superficiality, ostentation, hollowness, and even hypocrisy. The choice of the name *Francis* already gave more than a little clue for grasping this pope's deeply holistic vision for which everything that is genuinely human is cherished and integral.

For Azevedo, the underlying source for this expansive understanding of the Church's mission as evangelization is ongoing conversion of mind and heart that comes about most of all through prayer, spiritual discernment, and loving service of others. Ultimately, it is only through the cultivation of a deep interior life of prayer—the interior Christ—that the integration of faith and life, personal and collective, individual and social, will come about. Azevedo captures the urgency of the spiritual foundations for a truly evangelizing Church in the following words:

The very essence of Christian prayer consists in this vital articulation of religion and life, of personal faith and social existence, prayer which goes beyond practice and expression and transforms itself into a comprehensive attitude toward reality at the personal level and the first source of inspiration in life.[21]

The habit of prayer and the development of a strong interior life help make people free in order to follow Christ. The astonishing freedom that Pope Francis has exhibited in his words and actions is undoubtedly the fruit of the integration of faith and life through prayer that Azevedo links to inculturation. In *Oración en la Vida: Desafío y Don* (Prayer in Life: Challenge and Gift), Azevedo provides a comprehensive analysis of prayer and spirituality that sees prayer as the key for the integration of the secular, human, sociocultural, and economic contexts in which all people live today with the fundamental vision and inspiration of Christian faith. The *Document of Puebla* expresses the faithful's need for this kind of holistic spiritual integration by looking carefully at prayer in the life of Jesus himself:

> The Lord Jesus,...dedicated many hours to prayer under the impulse of the Spirit. He spoke to the Father with filial trust and in an incomparably intimate way. He gave an example to his disciples, whom he expressly taught how to pray. Moved by the Holy Spirit, Christians will make prayer a motif of their daily life and work. Prayer creates in them an attitude of praise and thanks to the Lord; increases their faith; confirms them in an active hope; it induces them to give themselves to their brothers and sisters and to be faithful to the apostolic task; and equips them to form a community.[22]

THE MYSTAGOGICAL ROAD OF POPE FRANCIS

With Pope Francis, one perceives a qualitative difference between papal communications in the past that have tended toward a style of intellectualizing and theological discourse to a fresh, new style that is deeply imbued with a more affective narrative discourse. Perhaps the word *mystagogical* best captures the style of Pope Francis's communication. Mystagogy refers to the process of a deepening of participation on the part of newly baptized Christians in the life of faith within their ecclesial communities and in the wider world. The retrieval of the early Church's emphasis on mystagogy arose after the Second Vatican Council in the context of the Rite of Christian Initiation of Adults (RCIA). The formation of active participants in the life of the Church and society takes place through a deepening of the person's relationship with Christ nourished first of all through the sacraments and the liturgy, especially the Eucharist, but also by community life and the habit of daily personal prayer (see *Sacrosanctum concilium* 64).[23] This may be linked as well to the Ignatian emphasis on discernment, making good decisions, or "discrete love" that is cultivated by a robust habit of daily encounters with the Lord in prayer.

Azevedo's approach to prayer and spirituality as key to integration of faith and life also links with the role of the pursuit of justice as flowing from faith. Interestingly, Pope Francis's predilection for the statement of Pope Pius XI ("Politics is one of the highest forms of charity") also dovetails well with Azevedo's insistence on the political dimension of prayer in any authentic Christian spirituality. Indeed, his closing chapter in his book on prayer in life could well serve as a lucid expression of Pope Francis's project for an evangelizing Church that some have characterized as radical in that it takes the people of God back to the sources in the Gospel itself:

> So the Christian should live on the level of faith as well as on the level of politics. He or she cannot confuse the two levels nor empty them of their respective identities. Nor can one opt to dissociate one from the other either by exclusion or omission of either. When translated into the reality of the lives of individuals and societies a Christian faith perspective on Jesus Christ interacts with, correlates to and integrates faith and politics without confusing them. One's education in and exercise of faith finds its major expression in prayer. Receiving and welcoming the Word of God is essential to this process. The Word of

God at one and the same time manifests to the one who prays the mystery of God and of human beings. In prayer and through the action of the Holy Spirit human beings deepen their understanding and acceptance of God's project regarding humanity as concretized in Jesus Christ. Thus the one who prays captures the consequences which flow from prayer, consequences for one's personal and social life, in one's relations with oneself, with the material world, with others, and with God.[24]

Therefore, the integration of faith and life occurs more than anywhere else in and through a robust prayer life and in a discerning heart that sees the connection between love of God and love of neighbor. By *neighbor*, of course, one means the other who is excluded, marginal, or most in need. This integration so insistently fostered by Pope Francis demands an openness to the signs of the times and courage to proclaim the truth of Christ while at the same time take action by engaging reality as servant not controller, with eyes and arms wide open in a generous attitude of both giving of oneself and receiving from others.

Chapter Six

AN EMERGING
PASTORAL VISION

A change in thinking about pastoral care and ministry is taking place throughout the world as a result of Pope Francis's astonishing example and evocative words. One of the main sources of this transformative orientation already mentioned has been around a long time, but Pope Francis is now using this simple but powerful tool to address the whole gamut of ecclesial challenges and situations, extending the method's use and bringing it to bear on pressing pastoral issues. The pastoral circle is a path from discernment to action. The steps are straight forward: insertion in reality or experience, analysis of this reality, theological reflection on it in the light of faith, and the development of a plan of action. It has remained a signature characteristic of the pastoral orientation of the Church in Latin America to the present day, even though some elements of the Church in Latin America preferred the dogmatic, deductive, top-down approach of the old Christendom. These elements did not carry the day, and the bishops together with Pope Benedict XVI at the Aparecida gathering enthusiastically reendorsed the pastoral circle method. They wrote the following:

> In continuity with the previous general conference of Latin American bishops, this document utilizes the see-judge-act method. This method entails viewing God with the eyes of faith through his revealed word and life-giving contact with the sacraments, so that in everyday life we may see the reality around us in the lights of his providence, judge it according to Jesus Christ, Way, Truth and Life, and act from the Church, the Mystical Body of

Christ and universal Sacrament of salvation, in spreading the Kingdom of God, which is sown on this earth and fully bears fruit in Heaven.[1]

As noted earlier, this methodology was also championed by United States' Latino Catholics in the *encuentro* processes as early as the 1970s and continues to inform the documents and vision of the United States Conference of Catholic Bishops (USCCB) as informed by its Subcommittee on Hispanic Affairs.[2]

THE PASTORAL CIRCLE

The pastoral circle requires dialogue with history and social science for the purpose of assessing the pastoral context and realities at hand, whether they be pertinent to the organization and service of a parish, care of families, general and religious education of youth, formation of adults, social ministries, or virtually any other pastoral need.[3] Pope Francis draws one of the implications of the pastoral circle method in a playful way referring to his preference for a Church that "goes out" to the margins and even experiences an accident to one that comfortably stays in the sacristy and "gets sick." The serious adoption of an inherently dialogical, engaging, and outgoing method today has much to do with the conscious focus of the Church on its identity and mission, which is to evangelize. Grounding one's vision of the Church in this method calls for paying attention to the "signs of the times" and to the gamut of critical factors of a cultural, socioeconomic, and political nature. Accordingly, bishops, pastors, and other church leaders must regularly focus on the reality of their ministries and works with an eye to new challenges that require energy, thinking outside the box, and effective pastoral planning.

Pope Francis's pastoral mindset is demonstrated in his talks and writing as archbishop of Buenos Aires in the area of marriage and family life. Some of them are found in a volume produced by the Pontifical Council on the Family. It is more than mere conjecture to think that Pope Francis's fresh approach inspired by the pastoral circle has had a significant impact on the Synods on Marriage and Family of 2014 and 2015. If one looks closely at his reflections, it is clear that they are informed by personal experience, social analysis, and deep compassion as well as by Church teaching. As a result, his thoughts on marriage and family life do not begin with a presentation of the beautiful ideals about marriage and family in Christian thought, but rather with the actual state of affairs. Francis talks about the actual status of family life in all its forms. Some of them are terribly broken and not living up to the gospel ideal. Yet this elementary and sad realization is not dismissed but rather is made the appropriate starting point. Pope Francis approaches matters of pastoral concern with feet planted firmly on the ground, not in the clouds. That is why, for example, he has insisted on the need to change the approach to marriages and families because the current one is in a state of crisis. The current approach to couples who live without benefit of a sacramental or civil marriage, for example, tends to simply exclude them. The approach to divorced persons who have remarried and not obtained an annulment is often to exclude them and, even more damaging, along with them, their children. Similarly, the prevailing approach toward persons who struggle with issues of sexual identity or who have entered into some kind of union with a same-sex partner is effectively to exclude. Pope Francis points out that "family catechesis has made an important contribution to forging a link between families and the life of the Church, but this catechesis is in crisis."[4] The pope inquires about the ways in which marriage and family life are undermined and proposes the need to engage people where they are in such a way as to encourage and nurture family life. He critiques the parish and tellingly observes that, there, "sometimes the predominant approach is more administrative than pastoral and promotes sacramentalization without evangelization."[5]

IGNATIAN PEDAGOGY

Of special note are the convergences and synergies between the pastoral approach for pastoral planning and what in the Jesuit world is called Ignatian pedagogy. Pope Francis's pastoral method shares many points of contact with both the pastoral circle and Ignatian pedagogy. This is a place where Pope Francis's exposure to the social and religious realities of his homeland and to the teachings of the Latin American bishops blends with Ignatian spirituality to shape a coherent whole. These methods have something in common: an emphasis on experience, reflection, prayer, and action. Faculties at Jesuit high schools and universities are formed in the key elements of this pedagogy. Students are formed to have an ethical conscience, and to be "women and men with and for others." Opportunities to integrate these social and ethical values are offered through exposure to Ignatian prayer, service activities, and to the *Spiritual Exercises* themselves in one of several formats. Attention to God's will and to the practical consequences of one's encounter with the Lord in service to others are among the most compelling results of the *Spiritual Exercises*. The service component provides practitioners of Ignatian spirituality with opportunities to experience God's call as mediated through others, especially the poor and marginal. Cardinal Bergoglio expressed admiration for certain developments in youth and young adult ministries in Latin America precisely because they have learned to emphasize the need to promote the agency of youth themselves rather than simply school them. Included in this is encouraging youth to find new ways to communicate the faith and give it life in the pluralistic environment in which they live and with which they are most familiar. This demands an ability to *listen* to youth rather than simply bemoan their unfamiliarity with Church teaching.[6] Such a pastoral approach flows from Pope Francis's familiarity with Ignatian pedagogy and its emphasis on developing personal responsibility and decision-making through prayerful discernment.

Importantly, the pedagogy that springs from the Exercises affirms that teaching and learning are instrumental. They are not ends in themselves but rather means for serving God and others. They are mission-driven. This pedagogy is centered on the student and adapted to him or her. The education imparted is organized and structured around some clear objectives for evaluation and accountability. Flexibility allows for the exercise of discernment, which presupposes freedom to make important decisions about one's own life and relationships with others and for making the response as personal as possible. Thus, the learner is motivated to self-appropriation and taking responsibility for his or her actions rather than to dependency on the teacher or guru. The pedagogy is open to improvement from any sources, methods, or techniques available and is, thus, eclectic. The pedagogy seeks to affect the whole person and induce change of attitudes and behaviors.[7]

Another example of how Cardinal Bergoglio's pastoral practice is rooted in the pastoral circle and in Ignatian pedagogy is found in his enthusiastic involvement with *Pastoral Urbana*, a fascinating movement among pastors and pastoral agents in Latin America. It seeks to develop new ways to evangelize in the predominantly urban settings of the Church throughout the Americas. One way to understand this new approach is to view it as a concrete example of taking the pastoral circle and Ignatian pedagogy seriously. *Pastoral Urbana* is a way of moving from traditional pastoral approaches to *missionary* ones that take into account new situations.[8] In an interview with *30 Giorni*, Cardinal Bergoglio responded to a question about his understanding of pastoral care in the Church by discussing the effectiveness of the parish as an instrument of the Church's mission:

> Our sociologists of religion tell us that the influence of a parish has a radius of six hundred meters. In Buenos Aires there are about two thousand meters between one parish and the next. So I then told the priests: "If you can, rent a garage and, if you find some willing layman, let him go there! Let him be with those people a bit, do a little catechesis and even give communion if they ask him." A parish priest said to me: "But, Father, if we do this the people then won't come to church." "But why?" I ask him: "Do they come to Mass now?" "No," he answered. And so?[9]

What the Cardinal Bergoglio was suggesting was that the parish church, itself, as an instrument of evangelization—the Church's primordial mission—is relative not absolute. If, indeed, the urban context is the primary one for ministry throughout the world today, there is a need for a creative pastoral imagination that goes beyond the traditions of the past few centuries. In the context of the United States, Cardinal Bergoglio's suggestion about reaching out through satellite locations in garages would perhaps take the form of satellites in strip malls or alternative arrangements for parish ministry like the Newman Centers at a university. Canon 518 of the *Code of Canon Law* actually provides for such "personal parishes" organized not territorially, but in terms of some other factor such as professional or occupational status, ethnicity, race, or something else.[10] The principal agents of this outreach, moreover, would often not be the parish priest but rather lay ministers or what Aparecida likes to call "missionary disciples."

The thrust of Pope Francis's view of the Church's pastoral life was captured well at the November 2014 International Pastoral Conference of Big Cities that took place in Barcelona. It was made up of urban-based pastoral agents, many of whom were involved in the elaboration of an effective *pastoral urbana*. After the gathering, twenty cardinals and archbishops who participated in the Congress traveled to Rome. Pope Francis gave them a brief but richly evocative reflection on their conclusions that dealt with the urgent need of developing creative pastoral approaches within the growing urban environments like the pope's native Buenos Aires, a region of thirteen million inhabitants. The concerns of this group were not at all new to the pope. Vatican Radio reported, "Pope Francis urged the bishops and pastoral care workers to take up the challenge of bringing the Gospel into big cities *with a profound change of attitude and renewed commitment.*"[11]

What does this "profound change of attitude" entail? The answer to that question is found to some extent in Pope Francis's involvement with a group of outstanding Latin American pastoralists associated with CELAM who have contributed to *pastoral urbana*. To grasp the pope's pastoral vision and the nature of the change of attitude it requires, it is necessary to take a closer look at *pastoral urbana*, which will be done in the following chapter. For now, a foundational approach to Pope Francis's pastoral vision requires more contextualization and reflection.

THE RECEPTION OF PASTORAL CONVERSION

The previous pages have highlighted some of Pope Francis's rich background and experiences that help explain his unfolding, often surprising vision for the Catholic Church in the second decade of the third millennium. Admittedly, it has not been easy for many, for traditionalists certainly, or even for some bishops, priests, and faithful who do not share Jorge Mario Bergoglio's roots in the particularities and peculiarities of culture, history, church, society, economics, and politics of Latin America. The traditionalist Web site *Rorate Caeli* and the Italian journalist Sandro Magister's blog provide clear examples of an overt pushback against the Argentine pope's project of "pastoral conversion." Bringing in a pope from "the ends of the earth," however, must mean something, especially if he believes, as he does, that the world is experiencing epochal change. Consequently, no longer can or will it be expected that the worldwide Catholic Church remain planted in the retrospective mindsets and attitudes of the European center that, if allowed to dominate, lead to turning the living organism of the Church into a stuffy, lifeless museum. What was peripheral now comes into sharp focus and, in some ways, it seems as if things have been turned upside down. There is strangeness, therefore, a difference, about this pope's way of proceeding. What would one expect given his antecedents and life experiences? What is different, however, is often irrationally feared.

One of the many novelties of Pope Francis's papacy is his overtly pastoral way of exercising ministry and leadership. At the heart of this pastoral orientation, as previously noted, is a straightforward regard for reality, the living encounter of persons, the flesh and blood humanity of God's People and the whole human race as the non-self-referential starting-point. In connection with this, one thinks of the contrast between the idealism of Plato and the realism of Aristotle, a contrast that has worked its way into Catholic thought from the earliest centuries of Christianity. Pope Francis opts for realism. The pope's message and manner, like those of any good pastor, engage experience and put reality—not ideas, ideologies, or even doctrines—in first place. It is not that Francis's predecessors had no regard for reality or pastoral needs. Their attention, however, was simply not focused on those issues to the extent it is in Pope Francis's papacy. Who could not see the extraordinary human qualities and gifts of St. John Paul II, the intellectual brilliance of Pope Benedict XVI, including his strong and brilliant assertion of Catholic Social Doctrine in *Caritas in Veritate*? The papacy of St. John Paul II, in particular, was a world-class phenomenon. As the unprecedented 2005 funeral service in Rome on the occasion of his death demonstrated, the Polish pope won the hearts of millions throughout the world, especially outside the Euro-American center. Nevertheless, the teachings and demeanors communicated by Pope Francis's immediate predecessors shared a distinctively cautious tone and were highly filtered by a fading ecclesiastical culture excessively influenced by a predictably Eurocentric vision of the world. How could it be otherwise? Their default drives, as it were, tended to take them back to the particular concerns and limits of the Church's exhausted European center of which they were outstanding products.

In contrast, Pope Francis has been and is treading new territory, and hence in the Western Church, especially in the milieu of those engaged and most deeply invested in ecclesiastical culture, there is something unfathomable about Pope Francis that leaves them puzzled and may cause them an unpleasant experience of disorientation and anomy: Where is this pope coming from? Where is he going? Do I follow him or dig in my heels? Cardinal Francis George gave voice to this frustration on the part of some bishops when he observed, "You're supposed to govern in communion with the successor of Peter, so it's important to have some meeting of the minds....I certainly respect Francis as pope, but I don't yet really have an understanding of, 'What are we doing here?'"[12]

MINING *EVANGELII GAUDIUM*

Perhaps the answer to Cardinal George's question can readily be found in *Evangelii gaudium*. Carlos María Galli, a close *Porteño* theological collaborator of Pope Francis, provides a cogent analysis of the pope's pastoral theology using *Evangelii gaudium* as the *"magna carta"* of this pope's pastoral vision.[13] By way of context, Galli notes that strong winds are blowing for the Church from two sources: the people of God and the Southern Hemisphere. While not proposing an explicit ecclesiology, there is no doubt that Pope Francis has one deeply imbedded in his mind and heart. He favors *the faithful people of God in history* as a term most expressive of how the Church can be understood in an age of new evangelization. He shows a marked preference for this term and often uses another one closely linked to it: *holy, faithful people of God.* This expresses a dynamic concept of a prospective rather than retrospective Church that is at home with the reality of frontiers, of ongoing reform, development, conversion, and change. Pilgrims do not have a choice. They must move on. They dream and hope—that is how it is.

What Galli notes about the strong winds coming from the South echoes the observation that Michael L. Budde made more than twenty years ago when he proposed the idea that the single most important change well underway back then within Catholicism was its transition from a First World to a Third World entity. One might say that now with Papa Bergoglio, the pastoral transformation Budde predicted has taken a quantum leap. Budde analyzed the shift particularly in terms of Catholic teaching on the economy and the Church's growing criticism of worldwide capitalism.[14] That criticism has been there since Pope Leo XIII's *Rerum novarum*. Nevertheless, the current pope's growing emphasis on this teaching disturbs not a few First World Catholics, especially neoconservatives who never accepted or ignored Catholic social teaching's longstanding critique of capitalism in the first place. This tectonic shift hailed by Budde, however, relates not only to economic perspectives, but also to cultural, social, religious, and pastoral ones. The arrival of Jorge Mario Bergoglio on the world scene is a clear demonstration of a real "change of epoch" manifested in a fresh stance for Catholicism toward the world.

THE JOY OF COMMUNICATING THE GOSPEL

Galli's first point is that *Evangelii gaudium* vigorously lays out a missionary and reformative concept of the new papacy that emphasizes the joy of the Gospel, "the sweet and comforting joy of evangelizing" (nos. 10, 80).[15] Like every legitimate reform in the Church's history, this one finds its inspiration in the encounter with the risen Christ and with the freshness of the Gospel itself, particularly in the *kerygma*, the proclamation of what God in his mercy has done for all humankind in Jesus Christ. This reform also insistently reminds everyone that being mindful of the poor is absolutely integral to the faith and life of the Church. The reform must manifest itself in following Jesus by opting for the poor. Moreover, there is something surprisingly joyful and catching about communicating this Gospel. The people of God involved in evangelization literally show it on their faces and witness to it in their attitudes and interactions with others. More important, they are also willing to make hard choices and sacrifices in carrying out that mission. In highlighting the importance of proclaiming the Gospel with joy that is deeply experienced, the pope is placing an emphasis on affectivity, not just intellectual assent, orthodoxy, or clarity, in one's intellectual grasp of the faith. Much less is this pope pushing for any kind of moralism or sentimentalism. The stance he proposes and exemplifies reflects a joy that results from prayer and reflection that is *integral*. This means bringing the gospel message to life through imagination and memory and through service of others and experiences that appeal to the emotions as well as to the intelligence. These become the material brought before God and mulled over in God's presence in the daily habit of prayer. So there is a regard for the spiritual journey of interiority and intimacy with the Lord, whereby faith and life, contemplation and action, are integrated. The joy generated by a loving, prayerful look at reality is the result of coming to terms with the reality of pain—one's own and that of the world—and the grasping by faith of the meaning of Christ's resurrection.

In choosing the name Francis, this pope signaled that a significant shift was occurring in how the Catholic Church today seeks to communicate its faith and its message, one that puts gestures, actions, actual events, and performance ahead of theological discourse and Cartesian "clear and distinct ideas." Such a drive toward enactment and performativity reflects the Latin American origins of the Holy Father's deep appreciation of the distinctive way the Americas were evangelized five hundred years ago and his high regard for "the faith of the people." This popular piety is part and parcel of popular culture, which, as Rafael Tello taught, is the primary incubator of evangelization in Latin America as well as other parts of the world.

GOD TAKES THE INITIATIVE

Galli's second key point refers to an insistence on God's prevenient grace. Pope Francis likes to recall a neologism—*primerear*—which means literally "to first." God "firsts" us, that is, before we can do anything to respond to God, seek reconciliation, or merit his love, God is already there seeking us out and loving us. Hence, the Church, like this outreaching, communicative, trinitarian God who loves his human creatures unconditionally, knows how to take the initiative without fear, seek those who are lost, and arrive at the crossroads of cultures and pluralism as indicated by Christ in the Gospel (see Luke 14:23). He invites whoever is excluded to the Lord's banquet. The pope links this irrepressible concern of God and of the Church to reach out in love to the "revolution of tenderness" manifested concretely in the mystery of the incarnation, God's becoming human in the person of Jesus Christ (*Evangelii gaudium* 88). Moreover, there is something Marian about this loving orientation toward reaching out and "firsting" his creatures. When the Church notes Mary's attitudes and actions as portrayed in the Gospels—in her Magnificat, her visitation of her cousin Elizabeth, her "holding all things in her heart," and in her concern about the lack of wine at the wedding feast at Cana—one discovers how it is that Mary is the living model or prototype of an evangelizing Church. Mary, the first Christian, is always reaching out like a mother and so must the rest of the Church.

Pope Francis has sought to express this strong pastoral vision in countless ways. In his daily homilies, he returns many times to his favorite themes that have a profound bearing on pastoral practice. He clearly acknowledges the Church's sterility that derives from allowing the desire to keep the commandments to weigh on us and take the form of neopelagianism, the notion that somehow one can save oneself by virtue of keeping the commandments and other rules, rather than counting on God's unconditional love and mercy. This lack of trust in God is the source of sterility: the idea that birth and life can somehow be self-induced, rather than received as a gift from the Other, a loving God. This new life and birthing is the work of the Holy Spirit, which has an unpredictable and surprising element about it. A Spirit-filled Church is not self-referential and has learned how not to be seduced by excessive concern about rules, regulations, legalisms, or even doctrines that never fully capture the mystery of God and may need further development. Speaking of the reality of an unresponsive, dogmatic attitude on the part of the Church toward the Holy Spirit, Cardinal Bergoglio once observed, "Our certainties can become a wall, *a jail that imprisons the Holy Spirit*. Those who isolate their conscience from the path of the people of God don't know the joy of the Holy Spirit that sustains hope."[16]

A NEW MOMENT

A third key for understanding *Evangelii gaudium* is to insist that the Church is living a new moment or stage in its evangelizing mission, one that highlights precisely the experience of witnessing to the ongoing joy associated with the Gospel's proclamation. This joy is seen literally in the lives of believers, and it has the effect of seeking to be communicated. It is through-and-through missionary in nature, however, seeking to go out in exodus, to be shared as a gift, and repeatedly sown in more distant fields wherever and whenever it can. As previously noted, Cardinal Bergoglio, gathered together with the Latin American bishops at Aparecida in 2007, observed,

> We are leaving behind one epoch and beginning a new one in the history of humanity....We are in the age of knowledge and information. Whoever possesses and manages these two elements is the landlord of power.[17]

The point being that there is a break—certainly not total, but yet very real—between how the Church has taken root and developed over the first two millennia and how it must proceed today as it moves into the third millennium. No longer is the Church the "landlord of power as knowledge and information," and thus the kind of power it wielded in the past is not so readily available. By the same token, the world, especially the paradigmatic culture of modernity, has brought about a substantial break in how culture deals with matters of faith. In this connection, the bishops at Aparecida point out,

> We are living through a change of epoch, the deepest level of which is cultural. The all-embracing conception of the human being, in relationship with the world and with God is vanishing.[18]

Already in the 1960s at the Medellín Conference, the Latin American bishops clearly saw that the project of Christendom by which the Church exercised formidable control over social and political life in forging a Catholic culture had come to an end. It was necessary for the

Church to now roll up its sleeves, seek how to effectively communicate its message, and negotiate with the world in new ways with many more added players in an age of pluralism and growing diversity. Continuity with tradition is certainly part of the way forward, but restorationism and traditionalism are not; rather, an adequate response to the challenges of the new epoch meant engaging popular cultures and the culture of the postmodern world as the crucible in which the drama of evangelization must unfold in Latin America and beyond. Moreover, the emphasis must be on openness and flexibility rather than on rigidity if the Church is going to engage cultures effectively in this new epoch. Even though this message was already heard fifty years ago at the Second Vatican Council, Pope Francis has brought this conviction of the Latin American bishops into the heart of the wider Church's response with exceedingly more vigor and incisiveness than ever before. Some elements of the Church continue to struggle with an uncomfortable sense of disorientation and anomy.

THE FAITHFUL PEOPLE OF GOD

The fourth key for understanding *Evangelii gaudium* is found in its insistence on the need for a deeper sense of human and pastoral agency among all the baptized. All the baptized must become protagonists, practitioners, not just recipients and spectators of God's outreach in Jesus Christ to the entire world. This was already noted with respect to youth, but the insight must be generalized to all areas of pastoral concern. Using the term popularized by the *Concluding Document of Aparecida*, Pope Francis refers to all the baptized as *discípulos misioneros* (missionary disciples). What is fundamentally at stake in this designation is the realization that missionary discipleship means becoming a man or a woman who lives with and for others (see *Evangelii gaudium* 273). There is, however, an aspect of this insistence on the outgoing agency of all the baptized that may be missed by some. One of the implications of this empowering of all the baptized is a need to rethink the Church's prevailing clerical paradigm. Cardinal Oscar Rodríguez Maradiaga, the convener of the Council of Nine Cardinals established by Pope Francis for the purpose of reforming the Roman Curia and proposing other changes, explains the equality of all the baptized in terms of the common priesthood:

> The whole church, the people of God, continues the priesthood of Jesus without losing their lay character in the realm of the profane and the unclean, the "cast out," a priesthood not centered exclusively in the cult at the temple but in the entire world, with a Samaritan praxis of justice and love. This priesthood belongs to the substantive plane; the other—the presbyterium—is a ministry *and cannot be conceived apart from the common priesthood.*[19]

In the same piece, Cardinal Rodríguez goes on to express the inappropriateness of the distinction between laity and clergy, a distinction that undermines the fundamental identity of all the baptized as missionary disciples:

> The clergy are neither "the men of God" nor are the laity "the men of the world." That is a false dichotomy. To speak correctly, we should not speak of clergy and laity but instead of community and ministry. (*Evangelii gaudium* 375)

Pope Francis follows the lead of the *Concluding Document of Aparecida* by insisting on the basic missionary character—what in Spanish is called *misioneidad* (missionariness) of the whole Church. One of the biggest obstacles to the realization of this missionary identity is the inappropriate distinction made between clergy and laity, which results in disempowering the vast majority of faithful from carrying out their proper Christian vocation to evangelize. *Evangelii gaudium* expresses the seriousness of Pope Francis's understanding of the baptismal vocation and identity. Vocation and identity revolve around a person's being part of a people, a real people. For it is in the living of relationships in families, churches, neighborhoods, regions, communities, and nations that persons negotiate meaning, especially ultimate meaning about which faith and religion are concerned. As a result, real evangelization of culture occurs more in this realm than it does in the strictly ecclesial context. This idea was already indicated by Vatican II's *Gaudium et spes* and expressed by Pope Paul VI in *Evangelii nuntiandi* when he noted that evangelization requires that the gospel message penetrate deeply into culture. Indeed, that evangelization occurs precisely when the Gospel *becomes* culture (*Evangelii nuntiandi* 18–21). What Pope Francis is adding to this insight is that the place where this inculturation occurs is not in some rarefied ecclesial context, but rather in popular culture itself, in families and human communities of every kind.

Consequently, the principle agents of evangelization are the laity, but if they are not acknowledged as such or even worse, dismissed or disempowered, the Church's very mission is blocked. Precisely in connection with this, Pope John Paul II in *Ecclesia in America* insisted that "they [the laity] are largely responsible for the future of the Church" (no. 44). Pope Francis goes even further and boldly asserts the following:

> It [clericalism] is one of the evils, one of the evils of the Church. But it is a complicit evil, because priests take pleasure in the temptation to clericalize the laity, but many of the laity are on their knees asking to be clericalized, because it is more comfortable, it is more comfortable! This is a double sin! We must overcome this temptation....Is he a good layman? Then let him continue to grow as such....In my opinion clericalism impedes the laity's growth.[20]

THE CHURCH IS MISSIONARY

A fifth key for interpreting Pope Francis is found in his insistence on a missionary Church that is primarily engaged in the transformation of the human heart and of the world. To speak of missionary outreach is to speak a great deal about a Church capable of taking risks and conceiving of its mission as related to every aspect of life. One of the implications of such a missionary identity is the effect such an emphasis will have on the Church's structures, ecclesiology, and pastoral practice. There is no question but that the missionary option implies the need for risk-taking. The pope has said as much:

> I prefer a Church which is bruised, hurting, and dirty because it has been out on the streets, rather than a

Church which is unhealthy from being confined and from clinging to its own security. (*Evangelii gaudium* 49)

Among other things, this emphasis suggests the need to relativize the institutional logic that keeps dioceses, parishes, schools, and other Catholic organizations from reaching out to the unserved and the underserved. It suggests the need to move at times beyond the tried and true structures that characterize the Church to new models of pastoral ministry. This, in turn, suggests the need to invoke the presence and work of the Holy Spirit in forming a creative church leadership that "thinks outside the box" rather than loyal functionaries and bureaucrats who merely replicate traditions that may or may not be outmoded.

POPULAR PIETY AND INCULTURATION

The sixth and final key, according to Galli, for understanding Pope Francis's pastoral vision is found in the people's popular piety and in the *sensus fidelium*. He uses the same words used by Rafael Tello—*affective connaturality*—to refer to the special capacity that the faithful, especially the poor, possess:

We need to approach it [popular piety] with the gaze of the Good Shepherd which seems not to judge but to love. Only from the affective connaturality born of love can we appreciate the theological life present in the piety of Christian peoples, especially among their poor. (*Evangelii gaudium* 125)

The pope goes on to say that expressions of popular devotion constitute inculturated forms of the Gospel and are "manifestations of a theological life nourished by the working of the Holy Spirit who has been poured into the hearts of the faithful" (*Evangelii gaudium* 125). In *Evangelii gaudium*, Pope Francis proposes that the faith of the people is one of the main sources of the inculturation of the faith, a concrete manifestation of how evangelization works.

Consequently, it should be noted that the first task given to the International Theological Commission by Pope Francis was to explore Church teaching on the *sensus fidelium*, a doctrine with a long pedigree but enjoying a relatively modest theological elaboration. In a December 2014 meeting with this Commission, Pope Francis admonished the group to "humbly listen to what the Spirit says to the Church." He spoke of "the lived faith" of the Church to which theologians must pay attention. Diverse points of view openly argued enrich the Church rather than harm unity.[21] Underlying the high regard Pope Francis has for the faithful people of God, one detects once again a connection with the thought of Rafael Tello regarding the role popular culture plays in evangelization and how it is the privileged *locus*, the place for inculturation and evangelization to occur.

TOWARD A SPIRIT-FILLED CHURCH

Another way to speak about the Church's pastoral vision, according to Pope Francis, is in terms of "evangelization with spirit." There is a strong pneumatological orientation in this pope's pastoral vision, one that integrates theology, spirituality, and pastoral care. The fifth chapter of *Evangelii gaudium*, titled "Spirit-Filled Evangelizers," carefully develops these three themes. According to Argentine theologian Virginia R. Azcuy, what matters here is the personalization or subjective appropriation of the mystery of Christ.[22] Contemplative spirituality is characterized by passivity whereby one allows the Holy Spirit to cry out in our midst and call God *Abba*! What is notable about Pope Francis's teaching is the way in which he integrates theology with a contemplative spirituality and pastoral sensitivity. The inspiration for Pope Francis's emphasis on spiritual integration derives from a persistent awareness of the Holy Spirit, a robust pneumatology that thinks of the Church in terms of a fundamental openness to communication from God and others and to a corresponding response to God and others. An Ignation emphasis on "finding God in all persons and things" is easily recalled in this connection. Encounters and relationships of every kind are at a premium in Pope Francis's world and thus the Church as people of God in history is always reaching out and susceptible to development and change, taking risks rather than clinging self-referentially to a circumscribed identity etched in stone. Indeed, the mere adherence to doctrine without the personal decision to follow Christ and experience his love interiorly makes the possession of knowledge rather than the attainment of relationship the focus of the Church's teaching and preaching. This is a mistake. Faith is more about trust than certainty. The pope refers to this as the temptation to gnosticism. Pope Francis insists that this is not Christ's way; rather, he proposes that "a spirit-filled evangelization is not the same as a set of tasks dutifully carried out despite one's own personal inclinations and wishes" (*Evangelii gaudium* 261). The suggestion is that the Church's mission must be integrated, interiorized, and made one's own. Thus, the evangelizer passes from being a mere spectator or perhaps, at best, an actor in God's play to a protagonist, even author, cooperating with God's ongoing creativity in time. Here, one detects an echo of the goals of the Ignatian *Spiritual Exercises* in which Papa Bergoglio was deeply schooled. Speaking of what will lead the faithful to become committed evangelizers, the pope says,

> The best incentive for sharing the Gospel comes from contemplating it with love, lingering over its pages and reading it with the heart. If we approach it in this way, its beauty will amaze and constantly excite us. But if this is to come about, we need to recover a contemplative spirit, which can help us to realize ever anew that we have been entrusted with a treasure which makes us more human and helps us to lead a new life. (*Evangelii gaudium* 264)

Above all, Pope Francis understands a Spirit-filled evangelization in terms of dialogue. More than anything else, the task of theology is to promote dialogue between the revelation received—the core Gospel—with cultures and the sciences. For him, the theological task for these times must be focused *outward* on encounters of every kind and on the pursuit of multiple ongoing dialogues. Such a posture is inherent to the Church's very mission. This, however, is now taking the Church beyond its Western paradigms into the heart of Asia, Africa, and Latin America. This outward focus into the heart of postmodernity requires the Church to shed its defensive skin and learn to dialogue with the whole human family, even with those who differ on serious matters of faith (*Gaudium et spes* 56ff.). Thus, the Church must confront changing knowledge and attitudes about issues of gender and sexuality with real discernment rather than assume a "circle-the-wagons" posture.[23]

The role of dialogue is also indispensable for the Church itself, for its *ad intra* needs and for pastoral care that reflects openness to the Holy Spirit. This was clearly seen in the October 2014 Extraordinary Synod on Marriage and the Family, when the Holy Father insisted on creating an unprecedented, free and open context for dialogue in which actual disagreements among the bishops and other participants were clearly acknowledged and brought out for public view. To be pastoral means to be informed about the issues, to seek for insight regarding causes and remedies. This means listening to various points of view, being well-informed. This is the opposite of the mentality of the bureaucrat who merely sees his or her job as simple enforcement of regulations. The image Pope Francis uses is quite pertinent: a field hospital in time of war. There is a kind of urgency and immediacy, a short-term view that must inspire a church seeking to function in a truly pastoral manner. That is why the pope has raised the issue of the care of divorced and remarried persons, of persons trying to live with issues of sexual identity, and of persons living in irregular relationships. These are matters that affect millions and millions of Catholics; and yet all too often it appears that the message being given to such persons by pastoral ministers is one of exclusion—"Good riddance!" The pope is reminding us that such a mentality and stance is simply not pastoral and, hence, not acceptable. Alternate ways to work with these and other situations that arise in today's world are urgently needed if the Church is really going to engage humanity in fidelity to its ecclesial mission. Pastoral solutions that respond to the reality, the needs, must be sought, but which also affirm the gospel teachings of Christ and authentic Church teaching, not the ideologically limited interpretations of one's favorite period or theologian.

This understanding of evangelization as depending on the internalized, committed response of personal faith to God's call and the development in the faithful of a capacity to give and take in dialogue highlights the difference between an approach to evangelization and religious educational development that emphasizes the adherence to doctrine, the clarity and coherence of the teaching, in contrast to the interior assimilation of teaching through formation. The approach that emphasizes doctrine and Church teaching may become rationalistic and often remains on the surface, while the approach that combines spirituality with pastoral sensitivity and outreach to others is, among other things, both affective and holistic. In other words, it engages the whole person—body, mind, feelings, imagination, memory, and will—much in the style of the Ignatian Exercises.

Much can be said about the rich background in thought and experience that Pope Francis brings to the universal Catholic Church at this remarkable moment of transition in her history. The emergent pastoral vision is one characterized above all else by a commitment to serious, respectful engagement with the diverse contexts—socioeconomic, political, and above all, cultural—and in a drive toward spiritual integration of the Church's response as the people of God to the challenges and opportunities of a new epoch under the Holy Spirit's ever-present inspiration.

Chapter Seven

IMPLICATIONS

By this point, you may be asking the following: Where is this remarkable epoch of change under the leadership of Pope Francis really taking the Church? What are some nitty-gritty implications of taking seriously this pontiff's remarkable calls for pastoral, missionary conversion? This chapter seeks to address this in a way that is still more speculative than concrete because this papacy is still quite young and certainly there cannot be a univocal, one-shoe-fits-all response to this pope's call for change. He, more than anyone, champions the Church's teaching about being a "communion in diversity." Nevertheless, based on my own reflections flowing from years of direct participation in the Church's life in many different capacities and venues, both pastorally and academically in the United States, it may be possible to draw a picture of some possibilities that may be inferred from the pope's refreshing vision.

FROM MAINTENANCE TO MISSION

Father David N. Power provides an insightful way to think about how pastoral ministry can fittingly be conceived today in an age when evangelization as understood by Pope Francis is absolutely neuralgic. In one of his last books before his death in 2014, Father Power, following the lead of Pope Paul VI's *Evangelii nuntiandi*, suggests that everything relating to ecclesiology and Catholic identity must be viewed first and foremost in light of mission.[1] The principle is that *ministry and order in the Church flow from mission and not the other way around.* This is essential. If the universal Church could or would grasp the implications of really putting mission—what Pope Francis in Spanish calls *misioneidad* (missionariness)—first, then a properly pastoral attitude would inform major matters of the Church's policies, for example, the proper care and ecclesial participation of divorced, remarried, LGBT, and other alienated people in the life of Christian communities. Matters of ministry, order, and pastoral care would find their underlying principles, rationale, or justification in the missionary nature of the Church and not in mere routine or lazy thinking, bureaucratic convenience, fear, exclusionary instincts of self-preservation, territoriality, or institutional logic—what Pope Francis jokingly refers to as "Customs House" mentalities. Mission means "going out" not "hunkering down," building bridges and not walls between people. In the Church, those struggling to do their best with the lights and possibilities they have cannot be dismissed just because they have failed or are not yet where the ideal as reflected in rules and norms might want them to be. A judgmental attitude is simply not pastoral, nor is a *maximalist* one that puts attaining the ideal first rather than encouraging at least a minimal move in the right direction. Pope Francis likes to repeat the phrase *Iglesia siempre en salida*: the Church must always be reaching out, seeking to heal, reconcile, and encourage much more than judge, dismiss, castigate, condemn, or exclude. The principle of gradualism that has been invoked as a way to move forward in working with gay persons or with the divorced and remarried is an example of a coherent approach that responds to the insight about Christ's and his Church's fundamentally maternal, or Marian, outgoing, and inclusive nature.

A kerygmatic attitude of mercy and a willingness to forgive and reconcile are maternal qualities that reflect the deepest nature of the Church. The Church is a mother! Christ is a Good Shepherd who focuses more on the lost than on the saved! To affirm these truths, however, does not imply a reversal in teaching or watering doctrine down, although modifications in practices and development of doctrine have been going on throughout history.[2] When the Church goes out, it may encounter or engage situations that demand a revision or development of teaching. There are those who quite reasonably believe, for example, that a serious look at matters of sexuality today requires further analysis, discussion, and discernment in light of new knowledge. Fidelity to the revelation received, the deposit of faith and the official teaching (magisterium), is one thing, but to bury one's head in the sand and fail to engage new knowledge and insights about sexuality and other important areas of life are quite another. The

Church's ministry to teach and shepherd the flock requires *competency* that does not derive from self-referential assertions of authority and the repetition of ancient beliefs, scriptural warrants, and formulas; rather, the challenge is to show how such beliefs and warrants may credibly engage human experience, scientific knowledge, and the world as it is. This was precisely the point Cardinal Carlo María Martini made rather vigorously in his last statement before his death in 2012 when he asserted that the Church is two hundred years behind the times![3]

Accordingly, one must ask questions about all the standard elements of the Church's pastoral life, its practices, methods, institutions, and organization, from the point of view of a missionary imperative. Ecclesial features and practices were clearly not given to his people by Christ in a finished form. Specific practices arose in time, have evolved, and must continue to do so if they are to respond to the dynamics of human history. The Church is the faithful people of God precisely *in history* and not in a regressive time warp, but rather in an eschatological journey that moves forward perhaps in a spiral motion more than in a directly linear one. Moreover, Church practice and ecclesiastical institutions regularly suffer the effects of corruption because the Church's membership and leaders are corrupt sinners. That is why the Church itself insists on the principle *Ecclesia semper reformanda*: the Church must always be reforming itself. It is one thing to assent to this idea notionally but quite another to take it seriously. Pope Francis is taking this need for real reform most seriously—he calls it *conversion*—and this can undoubtedly be disquieting to many, but the proclamation and prudential application of the gospel has always been disquieting! One must not forget that Cardinal Bergoglio was clearly given a mandate by the cardinals at the general congregation just before the papal election of 2013. They clearly realized that serious reforms were long overdue. Pope Benedict XVI's surprising resignation dramatically signaled the urgent need for reform not only in the Roman Curia but beyond that to the way in which the Church was being perceived, its credibility in the public arena, its finances, and several pastoral concerns related to marriage and family life.

There are several key areas of Church life that require analysis from the current pope's standpoint of renewal and reform. Like St. Ignatius Loyola in the *Spiritual Exercises*, this pope invites all the baptized to exercise a true *pastoral imagination* from a distinctly gospel perspective, an exercise that an ancient, deeply entrenched, and institutionalized Church—clergy and laity—may find very challenging and even threatening. Yet there is no question that the Church's vision of itself as focused on mission—the evangelization of cultures and the inculturation of the Gospel—demands ongoing review and revision along with pastoral-apostolic planning. Another word for this is *change*. The Church's practical reality, its life, must be viewed through the lens of Pope Francis's call for a thorough "pastoral conversion." What might this really mean? Four areas seem of particular importance in the effort to grasp the way forward for a truly missionary Church: (1) priesthood and ministry, (2) the sacraments, (3) certain neuralgic points of contemporary pastoral practice, and (4) faith and political participation.

THE COMMON PRIESTHOOD: MISSIONARY DISCIPLES

Pope Francis enthusiastically believes in Aparecida's vision of a Church that is made up of missionary disciples. The universal call of all the faithful to missionary discipleship is foundational to the thinking of Aparecida and Pope Francis. For the Church in Latin America, this vocation is captured in what the bishops called the *continental mission*. This formulation makes sense in Latin America, which is the whole continent of South America, the Caribbean, Central America, and Mexico. To speak of a continental mission for the faithful is to suggest a mission that goes well beyond that of one's town, region, or nation. The baptismal call directs the faithful outward beyond the boundaries of regionalism and nationalism, race, social class, gender, or sexual orientation. This universalizing vision, of course, also makes sense for the Church in every place in the world, not just Latin America.

The grounds for such a view are found in the Church's understanding of baptism from which flows the common priesthood of all the faithful. This is the vision of *Lumen gentium*, which insisted on the one baptismal call of all the faithful (no. 11). In light of the persistence of a negative clerical culture and generalized acquiescence of the faithful themselves with this ingrained clericalism, the Second

Vatican Council's vision has often been neglected in practice. In a 2013 address at the University of Dallas quoted earlier, Cardinal Rodríguez Maradiaga, one of Pope Francis's major spokespersons sometimes playfully called the "Vice-Pope," clearly reaffirmed the teaching of the Second Vatican Council as fundamental to the reform needed for the Church to truly move ahead with its evangelizing mission. Rodríguez Maradiaga emphasized that by virtue of baptism all the faithful share in a common priesthood that is the source of their vital identification with Christ himself. The ministerial, hierarchical priesthood flows from this common priesthood as a consequence and service. The common priesthood of all the faithful has a certain priority that has yet to be adequately appreciated in the thinking of church leadership and the faithful in general. This failure to appreciate the true priestly character of baptism is the source of a problematical dualism, a spurious division of labor that falsifies the meaning of the one Christian vocation. Speaking of this unhealthy dualism, the cardinal says,

> The clergy are neither "the men of God" nor are the laity "the men of the world." That is a false dichotomy. To speak correctly, we should not speak of clergy and laity but instead of community and ministry.[4]

Perhaps the stubborn persistence of clericalism is due at least in part to the failure to transcend the clerical-laity dichotomy that works against making the Church entirely evangelizing to its very core. Hence, an ingrained, convenient, dualistic way of thinking and acting works against the Church's most authentic identity and mission. Pope Francis no doubt assumes a Herculean task in attempting to purge this notion and correct a deep-seated way of thinking.

One of the consequences of the current clerical paradigm of the Church in the mind of many is a tendency toward self-reference that Cardinal Bergoglio denounced in his historic intervention at the general congregation just before his election as pope. When the Church is conceived as the bailiwick of a certain class of men who have "retreated" from the world and set themselves apart, renouncing wealth, sexual relations, marriage and family, such an arrangement does call attention to itself and can easily become "self-referential."

Rather than giving witness to the gospel of the Lord it is supposed to
be following, the Church in its leadership can unwittingly become
self-absorbed and even an end in itself, rather than an instrument or
mediation leading all to something much bigger, namely the reign of
God. The Church's focus must therefore be Jesus Christ and the
world he came to redeem, not the Church itself, much less the prerogatives of an elite. Cardinal Rodríguez Maradiaga puts it the following way:

> The calling of the Church, in the likeness of Jesus, is to
> proclaim the kingdom of God. Even Christ himself did
> not proclaim or preach himself, but the Kingdom. The
> Church, as his disciple and servant, ought to do the same.
> Her calling is to serve, not to rule. Pope Paul VI called her
> the "servant of humanity." She must do this service living
> in the world, herself a part of the world and in solidarity
> with it, because "the world is the only subject that interests
> God."[5]

An emphasis on the common priesthood of all the faithful and
their call to missionary discipleship of Christ offers the possibility for
a change of attitude and thinking about how the Church functions
practically. For instance, the persons responsible for its maintenance,
growth, development, or leadership are no longer limited to a few
who by virtue of seminary training and ordination are authorized to
lead; rather, the pool of ecclesial agents expands to include literally
the community of the faithful at least in theory. This means really
taking baptism seriously. Such an attitude toward the "ordinary" baptized is a long way from the old formula "pray, pay, and obey" so often
ascribed to the laity in the period before the Second Vatican Council.
While today's Church teaching on the role of laity has changed, old
ideas die a slow death and many sincere Catholics continue to think
mistakenly that the laity's role is peripheral, merely "collaboration in
the apostolate of the ordained."

The Church's work, its mission, however, is not narrowly defined
as merely cultic, "churchy," limited to the temple or parish church.
Hence, missionary disciples practice their discipleship *primarily in
the world*, in the workplace, the home, at school, in professions, as

workers, students, athletes, parents, single men and women, in business, economics, politics, in leadership of every form, and so forth. This realization is important in order not to remove from the ministerial priesthood the appropriate roles of leadership in liturgical worship, spirituality, and jurisdiction that properly pertains to it, or, even worse, to open doors for the "clericalization" of the laity.

If the world is to be evangelized, it will be so as the result of a Christian and catholic (universal) presence and engagement in all the strata of society and cultures as *Evangelii nuntiandi* teaches, not as the result of hunkering down as a remnant of the past or sect in some secure corner of the world. Nor will evangelization occur mainly in the church if, by that, one refers to sacred spaces made of brick and mortar. The world is the main place to evangelize and engage others with the Word of God especially understood as witnessing with one's life to the love of God and to the truth of the gospel.

Nevertheless, missionary disciples, especially women, are obviously called to serve the Church *ad intra*. This is the simple reality. They are the main day-to-day workers without whom parishes, Catholic schools, hospitals, and other institutions would simply not exist. Indeed, in the realm of pastoral care, women are *de facto* if not *de jure* the main actors or agents as preachers and teachers of the faith at home, as catechists, youth and young adult ministers, parish life coordinators, leaders in parishes, in parish and finance councils, small faith-sharing communities, and apostolic movements. In view of this reality, Pope Francis has insistently called for a greater, "more widespread and incisive female presence in the Church."[6] The point here is not to discourage men from coming forward to serve as priests, deacons, and other forms of ecclesial ministers, but to give needed recognition and authorization to half the baptized faithful who happen to be women, and call them to exercise their proper missions. The *de facto* reality of the Church in many places throughout the United States and beyond is characterized by the service and leadership of laypeople, especially women. Without this participation, a huge percentage of the Church's ministries would simply not exist. The path of recognition and leadership in the Church continues to reflect a strongly hierarchical *cursus honoris* that has long been out of step with realities on the ground. Pope Francis's focus on the fundamental equality of all the baptized is helping the Church move beyond such blindness.

In coming years, the demographics indicate that the ratio of priest to faithful will continue to widen—certainly in the Western world and perhaps beyond—and bishops will need to intensify the process of reconfiguration of ministries. In the age of Pope Francis, however, the growing engagement of the faithful in the life of the Church *ad intra* is not a stop gap arrangement awaiting a return to the "good ol' days" and the neat division of clergy from laity; rather, the emergent activity of the laity—more appropriately called missionary disciples—is the logical consequence of taking the teaching of *Lumen gentium* and *Evangelii nuntiandi* seriously. The exercise of the ministerial priesthood accordingly must take more into account the common baptismal priesthood and the *fundamental equality* of all the baptized while also respecting the particular functions that flow to each from the one Christian vocation.

With regard to the possibility of ordaining married men to the ministerial priesthood in the Western Church, it is now rather obvious that significant events are moving in that direction. Pope Benedict XVI perhaps unwittingly opened the door to this with the creation of the Anglican Ordinariate, which receives Anglican/Episcopalian priests, many of them married, into the Roman Catholic Church while maintaining many of the Anglican customs. Pope Francis has opened the doors even wider to the practice of admitting married men to holy orders. In 2014, he rescinded the prohibition of married priests from the Eastern Catholic Churches to function in the West. More pointedly, he reacted to a Brazilian bishop's suggestion that the extreme shortage of priests in his diocese be addressed by opening the priesthood to married men by saying that such a proposal could be entertained by Rome if the Brazilian bishops as a body were to gain some consensus among themselves about this.[7] Above and beyond gradual developments in the possibility of reestablishing a married clergy in the Western Church, Pope Francis's inductive pastoral method creates a basis for pursuing such a pastoral response: the practical needs and realities of the diverse situations of the universal Church. Such a pastoral method creates the conditions for greater freedom and creativity in addressing challenges while also safeguarding what is most essential in the gospel and the

Church's tradition. In this matter as well as in several issues pertaining to the two sessions of the Synod on Marriage and the Family, Pope Francis has instituted a method of discernment that requires frank conversation, the interior disposition of freedom (Ignatian indifference), and time to reflect and pray about these matters rather than settle them immediately.

With regard to the ordination of women, the picture is also changing but not so obviously as in regard to married priests. On the one hand, Pope Francis has made it clear that at least for now, the positions taken by his immediate predecessors will remain in force and the conversation on admitting women to the ministerial priesthood will not be entertained officially. On the other hand, the pope has indicated that the widespread participation of women in the Church must be addressed.[8] The suggestion that women might be named to the cardinalate (since historically it was open to laypeople and is not directly connected to scriptural warrants or the deposit of faith) received a quick response from Pope Francis that indicates that he is seeking some more appropriate way to recognize women's roles. He is quite wary of clericalism, however, observing that the proposal to create women cardinals lacks imagination because it assumes that the solution consists in allowing women into "men's-only" institutions. Is that the way to promote women in the Church, to simply replicate what the men do? This gender-neutral, one-shoe-fits-all approach to leadership in the Church may have the undesirable effect of imprisoning the ecclesial imagination in an ideology that gives supreme value to equality and the rights of *individuals* rather than the common good. Such proposals may unwittingly and needlessly tie the Church's responses to the structures of the past and to reductionist gender politics that conceive of women's roles in a way that dismisses complementarity and other concerns pertaining to the common good. Pope Francis does not follow the progressive or liberal "wisdom" about these matters; rather, he is a *discerning* pope and therefore he must attempt to create an environment of even greater freedom beyond political correctness and ideologies that end up censuring thought rather than liberating it. In the matter of promoting a broader, more incisive participation of women in Church and society as Pope Francis has affirmed, how might one think outside the box and imagine where the Holy Spirit is leading the Church and the world in an age acutely aware of the limits, foibles, and injustices of patriarchy and justly seeking ways consistent with the gospel to get beyond them?

Simply admitting women into the ranks of the ministerial priesthood may not be the response that best suits the needs of the Church today, even though theological arguments can be brought forward to support such an idea. Perhaps there are other assignations that offer women a better opportunity to use their gifts in service of the people of God more effectively and wisely. Limiting the ministerial priesthood to men, moreover, may be advisable at least in the short term in certain regions of the world where cultural attitudes warrant maintaining the status quo and where the Western world's approach to women's issues may be interpreted as a form of cultural imposition rather than true liberation. Could it be possible that in this and other matters such as the handling of same-sex relationships, whether "marriage" or civil unions, regional and cultural considerations may trump change at least in the short term?

As the common baptismal priesthood is emphasized in the spirit of the Second Vatican Council, women will continue to attain greater levels of participation in the Church's governance by means of diocesan, pastoral, parish, and financial councils, in tribunals and dioceses as chancellors, as head of Catholic colleges and universities, in councils in Rome, and as parish life coordinators. The scope of their effective leadership in positions of authority will undoubtedly grow, but not evenly throughout the world as the result of cultural factors. Appropriate options may be limited by routine thinking rather than a deeper analysis of what God may be asking in the changing but culturally diverse circumstances of women throughout the world. Consequently, the issue of women's ordination in a truly global Church will remain controversial, to say the least. Yet it is not exactly off the table and remains *de facto* a matter of serious concern.

PRIESTLY FORMATION

Pope Francis's call for pastoral-missionary conversion has serious implications for the entire Church but certainly for ordained leadership who are the principle gatekeepers for the people of God. The neuralgic point of reform of the clergy in this area relates to a renewed understanding of the *missiological* nature of the ministerial priesthood. The insistence of *Evangelii nuntiandi* and *Evangelii gaudium* on the Church as missionary in its entirety, to its very core, highlights the inadequacy of a cultic idea of priesthood that has gained traction among seminarians and priests over the past decades. Anecdotally, there are reports about the unsuitability of some seminarians for priestly ministry due to rigidity, and about bishops who, out of desperation for more priests, overlook the recommendations of their own seminary directors and formation personnel and ordain men not suited for this ministry.

Under the circumstances, it seems pertinent to ask about the status of seminary formation in this fluid context because candidates for the ministerial priesthood must willy-nilly adapt to new circumstances. In his visits to seminarians in Rome and messages to the pertinent Roman offices, Pope Francis has made no effort to disguise his concern about seminarians and priestly formation. For much too long, there has been a perception that seminary training may be contributing to an ongoing train wreck in which the Church's ministers lack versatility and resilience and find it difficult to adapt to pastoral realities. Pope Francis's remark about seminaries creating "little monsters" received plenty of notoriety.[9] The pope was emphasizing the point that neither the diocesan nor the religious order priesthood is the place to find a niche, a get-away from the messiness of the world, or pursue an ecclesiastical career. Accordingly, the fundamental documents of the Roman magisterium from Vatican II's 1965 decrees on the training, ministry, and life of priests to Pope John Paul II's apostolic exhortation *Pastores dabo vobis* in 1992 and beyond to the applications of these norms in the United States in the form of the *Plan for Priestly Formation* (PPF) will all require revision in light of the demands of pastoral-missionary conversion. The revision must find its primary inspiration in (1) an ongoing encounter with and missionary discipleship of Jesus Christ coupled to a real sense of the radical equality of all the faithful in the one baptismal vocation; (2) the evangelizing nature and mission of the Church (*Iglesia siempre en salida*); (3) pastoral conversion leading to a fundamentally inductive, pastoral orientation toward ecclesial praxis; and (4) the elimination from the ranks of the clergy (and laity as well) of "spiritual worldliness" as exemplified by clericalism. These four elements of a reform agenda for priestly formation, if taken seriously and acted on, have the power to renew the Church's ministry and priestly life in accordance with the guiding reform vision of the Church today. What appears to be in play is a reassertion of a more expansive *servant model* of priesthood, one that can truly "roll with the punches" over against excessively narrow *cultic* ideas of priesthood.

In recent years, generational differences between so-called Vatican II priests and current cohorts of seminarians have been noted.[10] These differences must be respected because they are reality, and willy-nilly older generations have to learn to concede leadership to new ones. On the one hand, the new generation is undoubtedly a product of the context of its gestation, which included broken families, social instability, a lack of clear parental direction and religious formation, along with a rise in individualism, narcissism, and a sense of entitlement. On the other hand, one notes a deep generosity and desire to give of themselves among many seminarians today. Some Catholic youth—seminarians among them—have found consolation in traditional religion's emphasis on order, orthodoxy, and certain moral imperatives. The end result can be an unhealthy tendency to build walls rather than bridges between and among the many diverse religions, cultures, and ideologies of a pluralistic world. Such an insular attitude obviously runs counter to authentic evangelization, which requires an ability to reach out to what is other, to listen and dialogue rather than hunker down with one's Catholic identity. Indeed, reaching out to other cultures, whether ethnic, national, or globalized like the culture of the modern, secular world, is part and parcel of an authentic Catholic identity. In developed countries like the United States, there appears to be a serious disconnect between the introverted dispositions of some seminarians, their excessive cultic understanding of priesthood, with what Christ and his Church actually expect of his missionary disciples, especially priests, in the first decades of the third millennium. There appears to be a somewhat widespread attitude among some seminarians of retreat from real engagement with the world, from openness to listening and dialogue with youth as they really are (that is, moving increasingly toward no religion at all), and from a truly missionary and servant (not to be confused with proselytizing) style of priestly life. This attitude shows itself in a warped interpretation of the priesthood that gives pride of place to filling a narrowly defined niche that fails to assume the broad range of presbyteral roles that include preaching, teaching, collaboration with others, concern for the poor, service, and community leadership.

Of particular importance for priestly formation is the integration of service learning or what is called *insertion* in Latin America into the seminary curricula. There is ample evidence that such learning experiences are among the most effective, life-changing tools in the educational and formational arsenals today. The changing attitude toward the participation of women in Church and society suggests that too much isolation of seminarians from contact and study with women is a deeply flawed approach, counterproductive, and dysfunctional with a vocation that requires familiarity, skill, and ease in building collaborative relationships with both men and women. Religious order priests in the United States often enjoy opportunities to study with and get to know women who are studying theology and ministry in the theological centers. In contrast, diocesan seminarians often find themselves in settings that are quite limited in terms of the presence of women, colleagues-to-be in pastoral agency and leadership. Women's ranks in leadership and service, for the good of the Church, will surely continue to grow wherever the newly formed priests will be missioned by their bishops. So how can seminaries and houses of formation equip new priests with formative experiences, knowledge, attitudes, and skills that will enable them to effectively serve in a Church that is evangelizing to the core? In the spirit of the Second Vatican Council and Pope Francis's reform, such a Church desperately needs the gifts and services of the faithful people of God—both men and women missionary disciples of the Lord. Ordained ministers must know how to recognize and maximize rather than disregard the presence and proper roles of all missionary disciples.

Additionally, among the experiences offered to seminarians must be exposure to the poor, service of the poor, because the poor more than any others can communicate God's love and presence to the fledgling priest. Consequently, provision for service to and engagement with the materially poor must be incorporated into the magisterial Roman documents on priestly formation. Moreover, it is urgent that concrete steps be taken by the body of bishops to regionally and locally adapt the formation of their seminarians in such a way that it more closely correlates with the need for "missionary priests" with sufficient versatility to adapt to the increasing challenges of parish and diocese. The extraordinary moment of reform that the Church is experiencing in and through the Petrine ministry of Francis provides a historic opportunity for renewal of the priesthood and of the entire Church. Priests as gatekeepers play an indispensable role in this remarkable development. Are they truly being prepared to support the Church's evangelizing mission? In this connection, one must ask about the quality of spiritual formation in seminaries and religious formation houses. Under the demanding circumstances of a Church that functions as "a field hospital," *affective maturity* is an urgent need if priests are going to successfully face the new epoch. The pluralism of today's world and the complex demands of church ministry today require more rather than less affective maturity among ordained ministers. This is a moment of crisis but also of grace that demands thoughtful, if not courageous, action by bishops and religious superiors consistent with the demands of pastoral-missionary conversion in a time of epochal change.

THE SACRAMENTS

The sacraments are at the heart of the life of the people of God. Pastoral conversion requires an ongoing revision of approaches to the preparation and celebration of the sacraments. Certainly, one of the most useful resources in the age of Pope Francis is the Rite of Christian Initiation of Adults. The RCIA provides an effective method for the preparation, reception, and celebration of the three sacraments of initiation—baptism, confirmation, and Eucharist. Two features of the RCIA stand out: the small community context in which the neophytes are formed, and the integration of the process in the Sunday Eucharist itself within the larger parish community. Of special note is the emphasis placed on reflection on God's Word and on the faith of the Church in community rather than in isolation. The methodology and spirit of the RCIA as one of the more outstanding products of the reform of the Second Vatican Council needs to be pondered and applied to the entire life of the Church. The small community and faith-sharing orientation of the RCIA suggests a remedy to the tendency toward anonymity rather than community so often found in the parish today. The effective linkage of the liturgical celebrations, particularly the Eucharist, to the life of the community is also paramount. These programs provide a context for group study, especially of Sacred Scripture, as well as prayer. As such, the RCIA model and other community-based educational and formational methods provide a viable context for building affective maturity in the faithful. Family-based activities are also very important as much of the reflection about the Synod on Marriage and the Family points out. These models are much better than the more limited schooling and textbook activities that often feed the mind but not the heart.

Parishes and ecclesial communities that undergo pastoral conversion must cultivate interaction not only in families where, unfortunately, conditions for evangelization and formation are not always propitious, but also within and among small ecclesial communities. Just as the African saying goes, "It takes a village to raise a child," so for the Church it "takes a community to raise a Christian." One must attend to what the word *community* means, however, and not simply assume that the large, often anonymous parish context meets those requirements.

Competence in intercultural relations, in attitudes, knowledge, and skills that foster effective communion among the bewildering number of cultures and languages present in many parishes in the United States today is a basic requirement. That communion must be closely linked to the Eucharist and to the liturgy, but in ways that are inculturated. In order to effectively achieve this, there must be more familiarity with what the Church teaches about the sacraments and how they are effectively celebrated in diverse cultures. The dream of "communion in diversity" will not come about by mere fiat, but by the grace of God and plenty of hard work.[11]

The sacramental, especially the eucharistic, life of the faithful has everything to do with the *community* in which the sacraments are celebrated. Their meaning is clarified for people within the context of personal relationships with God, among themselves, and with others. In the United States, the decline in the number of ordained clergy and the closing or combining of parishes has led to a policy of gathering more and more faithful into fewer parish congregations. To what extent can and does this approach run counter to the foundational need people have for some kind of real community experience in the preparation and reception of the sacraments? In the absence of viable community experiences, parishes can fall into an empty sacramentalization and fail to offer the necessary conditions for real evangelization. More important, does not the long-term mystagogical emphasis favored by Pope Francis imply the existence of a true communal base from which to continue the spiritual integration of faith with life?

The connection between the community of faith and each of the seven sacraments is absolutely essential, yet the practicalities of celebrating the sacraments often dispenses with making this connection in an effective, robust way. At the heart of the challenge is the lack of authorized pastoral agents, ordained or not, to facilitate the appropriate context for such an experience. This means preparing, authorizing, and commissioning people to assist and lead in the formation of viable communal structures wherever that can most fittingly occur—in the family, faith sharing groups, base ecclesial communities, the wider parish, or beyond it in outreach stations, associations, or apostolic movements. The celebration of the sacraments must be grounded in the broader life of the Church and of society, making the sacraments more than just isolated rituals and items of religious consumption. Pastors know the disappointment of meeting Catholics, even local parishioners, who relate to the administration of the sacraments as objects of consumption that must be distributed in the easiest and most efficient manner. When the parish becomes "a sacramental gas station," there is something wrong. There is no substitute for providing adequate formative experiences that help the faithful connect the celebration of the sacraments with their lives. Some priests, deacons, and laypeople, however, are not disposed to identifying, forming, and empowering more people to assume roles of leadership in the sacramental preparations and the ensuing mystagogical process. It is one thing to exercise responsible caution in the identification and formation of pastoral agents but quite another to lack the required energy and/or be excessively motivated by a need to control that limits people's access to the sacraments and other ecclesial graces for lack of ministerial leadership.

At the heart of the common call, which all the baptized have received, to serve as evangelizers or "missionary disciples" as Pope Francis calls the faithful, is a vivid and heartfelt encounter with the living Christ. This encounter presupposes some communal basis and encouragement in family life, in one's culture, and in a real community of faith. Christian spirituality, as developed in the mystagogical journey of faith, is of its nature ecclesial and communal, not private, in contrast with what often goes for "spirituality" in the developed world. The emphasis that Latin American Catholicism and Pope Francis give to the faith of the people—popular religion—relates to this point. Latin America Catholicism, as Rafael Tello insisted, developed outside the ecclesiastical context of diocese and parish. Catholicism mingled with the indigenous, African, and unfolding mestizo cultures of the New World to produce a distinctive Christianity that is certainly not perfect but is deeply communal and shared. As discussed in chapter 4, Pope Francis, following the lead of Lucio Gera, Rafael Tello, and the documents of CELAM, insists on the role that popular culture and religion can play in the gestation of faith, not only in the past but today and into the future. What this means is that the neat distinction made especially in the developed world between the seven sacraments and the Church's official liturgy on the one hand and the popular piety and devotions of the faithful on the other is not always helpful. This is a point amply developed by Jake Empereur and Eduardo Fernández in their pastoral theological study of the celebration of the sacraments in U.S. Latino contexts.[12]

Empereur and Fernández show how popular practices enhance the celebration of the official liturgy in countless ways. They also provide opportunities for expressing, deepening, and sharing the life of faith in ways that are accessible and palatable to the people.[13] Rafael Tello was of the opinion that the main place in which evangelization occurs in real life—certainly in Latin America, but arguably in many other places—is precisely popular culture. One of the defining characteristics of that culture is a common sharing of rituals, customs, and narratives. If popular culture is to be respected as a legitimate resource for evangelization and catechesis, then it must be connected in some way to the life of Christian communities especially in parish and diocesan contexts. In Latin America, this occurs in many ways through lay associations called *cofradías*, charismatic groups, schools, and sacred shrines like Luján and San Cayetano in Argentina and the sanctuaries of Guadalupe in Mexico or Aparecida in Brazil—to name just a few of these influential Latin American centers of popular

Catholicism. In the United States today, one might argue that the social media—Internet, blogs, Twitter, and so forth—offer comparable opportunities for communicating the gospel. How can these be marshalled in such a way as to create meaningful, human relationships and formation opportunities that advance the life of faith, especially in youth?

Much can be said about the fundamental necessity of grounding the Church's sacramental and liturgical life on popular cultures, which are shared communally rather than on a rarified ecclesiastical culture that can remain skin-deep and fall into Phariseeism. This is not to romanticize popular cultures that are also prone to superficiality, abuse, sin, and corruption. Yet popular culture must be engaged as an essential foundation for building faith and a genuine encounter with the Lord of the transfiguration. Jesus, who revealed his glory on Mount Tabor, "went down the mountain" and sought to go to where the people were rather than remain in splendid glory and isolation— enshrined, as it were, on the mountain-top as requested by the Apostle Peter. Pastoral conversion consequently requires an ability on the part of the Church's ministers to go out to the people, especially to the peripheries, as Aparecida and Pope Francis insist. It is not a question of proselytism, winning people over to one's group, but rather of communicating the gospel and allowing people freedom to respond as they will, as the Holy Spirit may lead them. Such an approach is truly other-centered and stands in sharp contrast to the self-referentialism and narcissism singled out by Cardinal Bergoglio on the eve of his election to the papacy as abusive and perverted attributes at the heart of the Church's contemporary malaise.

NEURALGIC POINTS

Underlying the pastoral implications of Pope Francis's reform is an evolving vision of ministry that befits an evangelizing Church entirely focused on mission. As church historian John P. O'Malley demonstrates, there are really two traditions of the priesthood. One conceives of the priest as having a niche in the parish church, as defined by parish-based ministries. This vision developed particularly after the reform of the Council of Trent, which, among other things, sought to reform bishops and pastors who were frequently absent from their respective ecclesial communities. In the popular imagination, priests came to be identified as parish-based ministers, not missionaries. The other vision of priesthood, however, is much older and linked to monasticism and the diverse charisms of religious order priests like the Dominicans, Franciscans, and Jesuits. These priests exercised a form of priesthood that maintained a strong spark of missionary zeal. The diocesan priesthood in practice often ignores the missiological aspects of ordination and settles for maintaining rather than expanding the parameters of the Church's engagement with all the baptized and beyond. Parishes often settle for a narrow, territorial approach that can become exclusive rather than inclusive and thus fail in its purpose to evangelize.

In the previous chapter, we noted Cardinal Bergoglio's conversation with pastors about the limited influence of parishes highlighted his concern that the tendency of parish priests toward maintenance and complacence about their parish be challenged. The missiological deficit among the clergy in the United States may be a function of overrating the parish. In the United States, parishes have thrived and have continued to experience considerable success in serving the religious and spiritual needs of many Catholics. Moreover, they exist in a variety of models and have shown considerable flexibility in how they function. The parish surely remains the locus par excellence of the Church's life, particularly as the center of true eucharistic communities. The parish also provides the "business plan," the practical way to finance church life. The point is not to disparage the parish construct but rather to insist that a truly evangelizing Church requires new models and "business plans" that reflect the Church's most authentic priorities and aspirations. Simply repeating what has always been done, focusing on mere practicalities, and pursuing the lines of least resistance are not acceptable.

In the age of Pope Francis, it becomes clear that despite its many accomplishments and stability, the parish like the Church itself, is nevertheless, only an *instrument* of evangelization, certainly not its target or goal, which is the proclamation and coming of the reign of God. The parish is an important means to an end, but in a world characterized by so much diversity, pluralism, and the physical, socioeconomic, and cultural transformation of people, its role must be adapted and relativized. This also means there must be a change especially in the way in which the ordained priesthood is exercised. No longer can the priest imagine his work as narrowly circumscribed to a niche, to a territory and to an unchanging number of cultic roles and tasks received from tradition. Moreover, collaboration with other missionary disciples who exercise pastoral agency in the parish and wider communities becomes a priority, shifting the entire parish leadership away from a maintenance mode to a dynamic missionary one that is deeply collaborative.

In connection with this, O'Malley notes the reality of two traditions of the ministerial priesthood in the Church: one for the diocesan clergy and another for monks and men religious. The diocesan priesthood came to be focused on the celebration of the sacraments particularly in parish churches, while the monks and other religious developed ministries in monasteries, chapels, hospitals, and schools. The reforms of the Council of Trent created a situation in which, increasingly, the priestly role was limited to parish-based ministries, to what O'Malley calls parochialization or "parochial conformity." He speaks of how the various provisions of what were considered and at the time probably were reform-minded provisions of church councils became "a massive force in transferring religious practice ever increasingly into the parish"—almost as into the only place of its legitimate exercise. Speaking of the parish from the Middle Ages forward, O'Malley observes,

> Even by the sixteenth century, however, and well beyond they [parishes] were only one institution in a vast array of others where Christians might find their devotion and engage in the practices of their faith.[14]

What exactly were the institutions other than the parish that provided a place to live and develop the life of faith?

> Among these institutions were shrines, monastery and manor chapels, the collegiate churches of the mendicants...the various confraternities or sororities or religious "guilds" that flourished in the cities and towns of Europe.[15]

The decrees of the Second Vatican Council on the priesthood unfortunately followed the Tridentine orientation that tended to collapse the understanding of priesthood into a parish-based conception. O'Malley and other writers suggest that this has actually done great harm to the priesthood and, more pointedly, to the Church's evangelizing mission because it tends to narrowly limit the more sanctioned and recognized ways to carry out ministries merely to the parish and not beyond them. O'Malley notes that, over the centuries, the design for priestly ministry has come to incorporate four elements: (1) ministry to the faithful, (2) in a parish, (3) in hierarchical union with the bishop, and (4) with a warrant for ministry coming from ordination to the diaconate or presbyterate. This four-part template captures how the priesthood functions for diocesan priests in particular, especially since the time of the Council of Trent. This pattern, however, does not actually conform so neatly or clearly to the situations and practices of the "regular clergy," as the religious order priests have been called, at least as exercised in past centuries but, one might argue, even today.

This concern is particularly pertinent to the Church in the United States, which has had a very successful historical experience of parish and has invested considerable effort into the organization, standardization, and maintenance of the parish institution in various forms. In contrast, the historical and contemporary experiences of and attitudes toward the parish in many other places throughout the Catholic world have been and still are notably different. The case of Latin America stands out. The evangelization that took place there almost five centuries ago was almost entirely the work of the Augustinians, Dominicans, Franciscans, and Jesuits. The more expansive understanding of priesthood characteristic of the religious orders was the norm and in many ways remains the norm even though the diocesan clergy has certainly grown and leads the way today. Nevertheless, institutions originally and even still associated with religious orders—shrines, collegiate churches, confraternities, and religious guilds of various sorts—are quite prevalent. Additionally, strong apostolic movements like the Charismatic Renewal, the Christian Family Movement, the Cursillo, and base ecclesial communities function as the main place for many people in which the life of faith is celebrated. All of this tends to relativize the place of parish in the scheme of things in Latin America, both historically and today. Pope Francis speaks eloquently of the parish and links it to the formation of strong families, but he is not speaking necessarily about the experience of parish in the United States with its strong institutional profile and particularity.

The pastoral conversion proposed by Pope Francis requires a change in thinking and attitude about the parish, particularly in the United States. The conversation of Cardinal Bergoglio with some of his pastors suggests that parishes are sometimes rather limited in their ability to reach certain people. He expresses his desire for a more expansive and robust idea of how the Church and its ministers must work in order to really connect with groups that the parish in its various modalities cannot or will not reach. In connection with this, the comment of Cardinal Reinhard Marx, one of the nine cardinals on the special council established by Pope Francis, was especially pertinent. At a conference he gave at Stanford University, he was asked how more people could be brought into the Church. A journalist working for the Italian daily, *La Stampa*, reported that Marx "flipped the question" and responded,

> How can we make the Gospel the most important revelation in the history of humanity, a part of society's future? The Gospel is not to be kept inside the Church: it should be shared and proclaimed aloud for the good of everyone.[16]

Cardinal Marx's response beautifully reflects the mindset of Pope Francis, one characterized by counterintuition, magnanimity, and openness in the spirit of section 22 of St. Ignatius's *Spiritual Exercises*, where Ignatius insists that putting a good interpretation of the thought of the other is a prerequisite for growth in spirituality rather than being defensive, closed, or hell-bent on winning others over to one's own ideas. This mentality is the absolute antithesis of sectarianism, which the Catholic Church has decried throughout its history but into which elements of the Church have succumbed more than once.

FAITH AND POLITICAL PARTICIPATION

The significance for the entire Church of a pope "from the ends of the earth" who is rooted in the thought and concerns of "the periphery" is hard to exaggerate. A process of decentralization conceived and carried out by this Argentine pope is taking place before the eyes of the whole world. Among other things, that decentralization has the effect of reducing the influence that the Western world, particularly the United States and Europe, have on the worldwide Catholic Church, specifically the Church in Rome. Perhaps nothing illustrates this significant development more than the changing face of the College of Cardinals. Additionally, Papa Bergoglio's origins in a lower middle class, immigrant community are also significant. Pope Francis is not only positioned to advocate for "the excluded within the Church"; he has begun from the first moments of his papacy to raise the global reality of inequality, discrimination, exclusion, ecological degradation, and injustice for the entire world to acknowledge and see.

What is particularly distinctive about this pope, however, is his absolute insistence on political participation and commitment to social justice that flow from faith and love and not ideology. The experience of Latin America in the contentious decades of the 1970s and '80s provided lessons about the limits of ideologies of either the right or the left. Jorge Mario Bergoglio learned these lessons. In bracketing social justice advocacy and service of the poor from ideology, he seeks to ground concern for the poor in faith and in love more than in morality or even rationality. Christian concern for the poor is, after all, grounded most of all on faith, that is, on what God has revealed to the Church about himself in the Bible, especially in the Gospels, and in the Church's traditions.[17] This pope seeks more than anything else to motivate others to serve the poor spiritually and materially but also to learn from them. Witness and attraction are the single most important instruments of evangelization, and the most effective examples of that are found in concern for and service of the poor. Pope Francis has communicated this point consistently from his choice of simpler living arrangements, simpler vehicles in which to travel, and less ostentation in papal rituals, to appointing an active almoner who would reach out to the poor of Rome on the pope's behalf. As a result, the needs of the homeless around the Vatican for common necessities like a place to shower, sleeping bags, and a good meal are being addressed.

The pope's frequent affirmations of Catholic social teaching have captured much attention, from his statements to the European

Union to his messages to various sections of the United Nations and other international agencies. He has highlighted the growing gap of socioeconomic inequality in so many parts of the world including the more affluent nations like the United States and Europe. He has raised the issue of the "globalization of indifference," the disturbing phenomenon of growing ignorance or neglect of the dehumanizing and violent situations of various kinds in so many places in the world. An encyclical on the ecology and stewardship of the earth planned for publication in 2015 will align the Church more emphatically with forces in the world seeking to take responsibility for the degradation of the earth, climate change, and especially the particularly appalling effects of these realities on the poor and vulnerable.

The obvious conclusion to be drawn about the linkage between faith and the pursuit of social justice under this pope's leadership is that his clear, prophetic orientation may go far in reversing the tendency to separate faith from matters of social and civic concern. For Catholics, such a separation is simply unthinkable. That was brought home in one of Pope Francis's famous homilies:

> It is not true that a good Catholic doesn't meddle in politics....A good Catholic meddles in politics, offering the best of himself, so that those who govern can govern. But what is the best that we can offer to those who govern?[18]

At the same time, this pope's dislike of ideology may help the Church communicate the prophetic message, the option for the poor, in ways that do not confuse the gospel message with partisan political ideologies of the left or the right. In the United States' context, there is plenty of room to criticize both major political parties on any number of matters pertaining to the disregard for human dignity and the call of Catholic social teaching for justice. Nevertheless, official Church commentary on socioeconomic and public policy matters from this pope, from bishops, local pastors, and socially committed missionary disciples will undoubtedly continue to receive serious pushback from entrenched sources, some of them claiming to be more Catholic than the pope.

The papacy of Pope Francis, however, has generated an enormous amount of support due to the transparency, skill, and dispatch with which it has proceeded. Pope Francis has proven himself to be a superb administrator and inspiring leader. He has articulated the connection between the Catholic Church's spiritual mission to preach love of God and neighbor along with its material, visible consequences in the real world. While respecting Catholic tradition, especially the unique role played by the Bishop of Rome in the Catholic Church and on the world scene, he has demonstrated an astonishing adeptness at adapting the institution to new conditions in which Europe and the Western world are no longer the centers of power. He is striving to bring the peripheries into the center and transform the Church's mood and attitudes toward its mission and identity. He brings pastoral sensitivity, imagination, and gusto to his ministry and leads by example. The tone and contours of the Church's mission to proclaim the gospel with a delightful freshness come into clearer focus in the context of dynamic, epochal changes. Pope Francis's call to pastoral conversion is here to stay. The appealing vision of a Church "always going out" both challenges and motivates the faithful people of God in history, and the direction in which he is taking the universal Church is becoming irreversible.

CONCLUSION

What emerges from this tentative effort to explore at greater depth the vision and direction of Jorge Mario Bergoglio, otherwise known as Francis, Bishop of Rome, is a complex, heartening, and intriguing picture. He is an inspired man with a calling to lead, a man of governance and unusual grit and courage. In a matter of months, he succeeded in changing the mood and tone of the Church both internally and in its relationship with the wider world. At the core of this change of mood and tone is a clear shift away from a dogmatic stance to a more practical one, from doctrine to praxis. As has been noted by many including Pope Francis himself, the new approach is not a matter of denying or changing doctrines, even though doctrines obviously do undergo development; rather, it is a matter of first engaging experience or reality with an attitude of outreach, with a disposition aligned with God's mercy, with as much openness, acceptance, and hope as possible.

The Canadian Jesuit philosopher Bernard Lonergan provides a way to view this shift toward a receptive, pastoral orientation. He views the process as a movement from a classical consciousness in which one emphasizes the static, fixed nature of things, to a critical, historical awareness and worldview in which the dynamic, fluid aspects of reality are emphasized.[1] Pope Francis's inductive pastoral methodology gives pride of place to reality and its broader contextualization, to events on the ground. Taken seriously, the pastoral circle see-judge-act methodology adopted by Cardinal Joseph Cardijn almost a century ago has become more of a real "game changer" than ever. One of the consequences, for example, is the Church's movement away from a judgmental stance toward people who experience divorce, homosexuality, living together as man and wife without benefit of marriage, and same-sex marriages. Catholic teaching, particularly the Gospels, undoubtedly provides important principles for critical assessment of how people are doing in living up to the standards of faith. Papa Bergoglio begins with recognition of whatever is good in an otherwise questionable situation, for instance, the divorced and remarried person who has not received an annulment but nevertheless seeks to receive the Eucharist at Mass. This person is truly seeking God and this is praiseworthy. How may this person remain realistically connected to the ecclesial community? Francis seems to be suggesting that the Church start there, with a *constructive* disposition, rather than with what is lacking in this situation, namely, an official declaration of nullity from a diocesan marriage tribunal. Similarly, with persons struggling with a same-sex orientation, they are God's children and like everyone else are sinners. Are they excluded from the Church because they do not live up to the ideal? Perhaps they will in time live up to the ideal, but who ever does completely? What about transsexual persons who in the past were not encouraged to admit their situation, were rebuffed and scorned? What would Jesus do? Spurn these people whom God surely loves merely because their sexuality is ambivalent? Would not the Lord show concern and acceptance of people who are in a difficult situation and are doing what they can to address it? One might ask a similar question about the children of same-sex couples in Catholic schools. Are there sufficient reasons to ban such children from Catholic schools as has occurred at times in the United States just because their parents do not live up to the ideal of Christian marriage? These are just some of the fascinating and vexing issues that Pope Francis seeks to address with a renewed pastoral lens. Underlying the approach is the change in method that emphasizes doctrine over the existential realities and the dynamic nature of human life.

More pertinent in connection with this, however, is what Francis calls "the revolution of tenderness," the kerygmatic emphasis on God's mercy, nearness, and love. This principle, which is profoundly evangelical, provides a basis for thinking of the Church as inclusive rather than exclusive. This, in turn, connects with Pope Francis's understanding of the dynamic of evangelization as centrifugal—impelling the Church outward to the geographical, social, economic, or existential margins.

Corresponding to the shifting pastoral orientation of this pope is an equally transformative approach to communications. Despite his advanced age, Pope Francis knows well how to communicate effectively with the world, including today's youth and young adults. He regularly presents his stimulating thought in the form of appealing gestures and stories as well as in concepts, ideas, or discursive reasoning. The result is a rather successful communication with the broader world that captures imaginations and moves hearts. Of the many graphic images of this pope, few were as moving as his embrace and kiss of the terribly disfigured man suffering from what appeared to be elephantiasis. The photo of his washing the feet of youth in a Roman prison, among them a Muslim woman, communicated the gospel message more effectively than any encyclical ever could. Pope Francis understands well the principle taught centuries ago by St. Thomas Aquinas in *Summa Theologiae* that effective preaching and teaching require knowledge and insight about the way in which the Christian message is received by one's audience. Medium is arguably as important as content, and "The medium is the message," as Marshall McLuhan famously contended.[2]

One detects in Pope Francis's approach a strong concern for spirituality, which helps the Christian faithful, the people of God, integrate the gospel with life. Thus, his communications show appreciation for the role of affectivity in moving and motivating persons toward true conversion or transformation. Indeed, one might refer to what he has accomplished in just a few years as an *affective revolution*. He leads by example with his own staff at the Vatican by organizing a yearly, silent Lenten retreat and requiring everyone on staff to attend. The Christmas talk of 2014 was an "examination of conscience" for the curia in which he listed fifteen ills or sources of corruption for officials of the curia. This opportunity for spiritual reflection was not well received by some who were not used to this kind of nitty-gritty exhortation.[3]

In terms of his understanding of the Church, Pope Francis has shown a preference for the term "faithful people of God in history." This is a way of looking at the Church that emphasizes the equality of all members and their common responsibility and mission. It is also a less hierarchical way of thinking about the Church than Catholics have been used to, one that empowers the dynamic engagement of all in the proclamation of the good news of Jesus Christ by attending to the "signs of the times," by paying attention to what is happening in the real world. The term *people of God* evokes the story of the Exodus and the essentially prophetic and liberating elements of the people of God's experience and identity. This requires attention to matters of social justice, especially concern for the poor and excluded. The people of God, however, are a pilgrim people, and thus their journeying is a truly communal endeavor with a movement and purposefulness that goes beyond human history. The journey reaches fulfillment in the final coming of Christ, what theologians call the *eschaton*. Consequently, the Church as people of God in history has a clearly *transcendent* purpose that escapes the confines of history in the encounter with the God who is always more—*Deus semper mayor*.

Pope Francis's conception of the Church may seem to relativize it somewhat as an institution. His rejection of any kind of proselytism is grounded on the notion that it is through witness and attraction that the Church moves ahead on its journey, but the point of this witness and attraction must be the reign of God, not the Church itself. Membership is not so important as hearing and acting on God's message of love as embodied in the reign of God. For when the Church makes itself an end in itself, it sows the seeds of the destructive self-reference that Cardinal Bergoglio critiqued in his now famous four-minute speech to the general congregation on the eve of the conclave that elected him pope. Of particular note are the ecumenical and interreligious benefits of such a nuanced view of the Church's mission. By insisting on the inappropriateness of self-reference and proselytism, Pope Francis has contributed to the creation of a climate of receptivity, mutual respect, and dialogue, a true give-and-take, among the Christian denominations and religions of the world. This strong ecumenical and interreligious orientation is nourished by Pope Francis's insistence on the notion that the faithful people of God in history constitute a communion in diversity, in differences, rather than in uniformity.

Can anyone now deny that with Pope Francis, worldwide Catholicism is turning a corner and that the vista before our eyes is vast, exciting, and challenging? But the corner is being turned! Epochal change has come to the world Church under the astonishing leadership of the pope from "the ends of the earth." Now we see a renewed Church arising—one that is "bruised, hurting and dirty because it has been out on the streets, rather than a Church which is unhealthy from being confined and from clinging to its own security" (*Evangelii gaudium* 49).

NOTES

Introduction

1. Pope Francis, *Evangelii gaudium*, The Joy of the Gospel (Boston: Pauline Books and Media, 2013), no. 52.

2. See Massimo Faggioli, *Vatican II: The Battle for Meaning* (New York: Paulist Press, 2012).

3. Episcopal Conference of Aparecida, *Concluding Document: V General Conference of the Bishops of Latin America and the Caribbean* (Washington, DC: USCCB Publishing, 2008).

Chapter One: Setting the Stage

1. Xavier Pikaza, "El Blog de X. Pikaza," July 16, 2014, see http://blogs.periodistadigital.com/xpikaza.php.

2. Elisabetta Piqué, *Francis: Life and Revolution* (Chicago: Loyola Press, 2015).

3. The term *Porteño* refers to people from Buenos Aires, the great port city of Rio de la Plata, and their thriving culture.

4. Pope Francis's magna carta *Evangelii gaudium* (*EG*) highlights both the Virgin Mary's role as model of and for evangelization and of concern for social justice as integral to the Church's mission. On Mary, see *EG* 284–88, and on social concerns, see all of chapter 4.

5. The "Gregorian" refers to the Pontifical Gregorian University in Rome founded by St. Ignatius Loyola.

6. International Theological Commission, *Sensus Fidei in the Life of the Church* (Rome: Editrice Vaticana, 2014).

7. Sergio Rubin and Francesca Ambrogetti, *El Jesuita: Conversaciones con el Cardenal Jorge Bergoglio, SJ* (Buenos Aires: Vergara, 2010), 117.

8. Roberto Cortés Conde, *The Political Economy of Argentina in the Twentieth Century* (New York: Cambridge University Press, 2009), 2–10.

9. In a September 16, 2013, speech as reported by Vatican Radio, Pope Francis said, "Politics, according to the Social Doctrine of the Church, is one of the highest forms of charity, because it serves the common good." This assertion also echoes a teaching of the twelfth-century Spanish-Jewish philosopher Maimonides regarding levels of charity, or *tzedekah* in Hebrew.

10. In a Spanish-language article titled "El Método Bergoglio para Gobernar" (Bergoglio's method for governing) in *La Nación*, Carlos Pagni wrote, "His [Bergoglio's] friends define him as a strategist who never says anything just for the sake of saying it nor does anything just for the sake of doing it....Francisco pays close attention to civilian politics as revealed by his dialogues with the leadership of all the political parties." Current author's translation from the original Spanish. See Carlos Pagni, La Nación, March 21, 2013.

11. Elisabetta Piqué, *Francisco: Life and Revolution* (Chicago: Loyola Press, 2014), 59.

12. *Media Matters* blog, "Pope Francis Rebukes 'Marxist' Attack from Rush Limbaugh and Conservative Media," December 15, 2013, http://mediamatters.org/blog/2013/12/15/pope-francis-rebukes-marxist-attack-from-rush.

13. Ricardo Julio Jaen, *Opinión*, March 15, 2014.

14. Cortés Conde, *The Political Economy*, 2–10.

15. Austen Ivereigh, *The Great Reformer: Francis and the Making of a Radical Pope* (New York: Henry Holt and Company, 2014), 89.

Chapter Two: Jesuit Roots

1. John W. O'Malley, *The Jesuits: A History from Ignatius to the Present* (New York: Rowman and Littlefield, 2014), 88–96.

2. David Lonsdale, "Ignatian Spirituality," in *The New Westminster Dictionary of Christian Spirituality*, ed. Philip Sheldrake (Louisville: Westminster John Knox Press, 2005), 354–56.

3. Enrique Hernán García, *Ignacio de Loyola* (Caracas, Venezuela: Taurus, 2013), 210.

4. *Finding God in All Things: A Marquette Prayer Book* (Milwaukee, WI: Marquette University Press, 2009).

5. De Paul University Center for World Christianity and Theology, "New World Pope: Pope Francis and the Future of the Church," Conference, February 8, 2014, see http://las.depaul.edu/cwcit.

6. Joseph Tetlow, *Choosing Christ in the World* (St. Louis: Institute of Jesuit Sources, 2000).

7. David Lonsdale, *Listening to the Music of the Spirit, the Art of Discernment* (Notre Dame, IN: Ave Maria Press, 1993).

8. George Aschenbrenner, "Consciousness Examen," *Review for Religious* 31 (1972): 14–21; see also Howard Gray, "Examination of Conscience/Consciousness," *The New Westminster Dictionary of Christian Spirituality*, ed. Phillip Sheldrake (Louisville: Westminster John Knox Press, 2005), 292–93.

9. Pope Francis's words to priests in Caserta on July 29, 2014. See http://www.zenit.org/en/articles/pope-s-dialogue-with-priests-in-caserta.

Chapter Three: The Latin American Ethos of Renewal

1. Faggioli, *Vatican II*, 53–55 (see intro., n. 2).

2. Francis McDonagh, ed., *Dom Helder Camara: Essential Writing* (Maryknoll, NY: Orbis Books, 2009), 11–36.

3. Frans Wijsen, "The Practical-Theological Spiral," in *The Pastoral Circle Revisited*, ed. Frans Wijsen, Peter Henriot, and Rodrigo Mejía (Maryknoll, NY: Orbis Books, 2005), 108–26.

4. Virginia Azcuy in *Escritos Teológicos-pastorales de Lucio Gera*, ed. V. R. Azcuy, C. M. Galli, and M. González (Buenos Aires: Libros Agape, 2006), 23.

5. "Scannone, SJ, Explica la Teología del Pueblo del Papa Francisco," February 13, 2015, http://www.jesuitas.es/inex.php?view.

6. Ibid.

7. Ivereigh, *The Great Reformer*, 95 (see chap. 1, n. 15). See also Fernando Boasso "El Contexto Histórico Eclesial," in *Escritos Teológico-pastorales de Lucio Gera*, ed. V. R. Azcuy, C. M. Galli, M. González (Buenos Aires, Agape Libros, 2006), 1:175–77.

8. Lucio Gera, "Conference for the Week on Popular Religiosity in Latin America organized by CELAM," August 20–26, 1976.

9. See V. R. Azcuy, C. M. Galli, M. González, eds. *Escritos Teológico-pastorales de Lucio Gera* (Buenos Aires: Agape Libros, 2006), 1:121–65.

10. Gera, "Conference for the Week on Popular Religiosity."

11. Ivereigh, *The Great Reformer*, 115 (see chap. 1, n. 15).

12. Enrique Ciro Bianchi, *Pobres en este Mundo, Ricos en la Fe* (Buenos Aires: Libros Agape, 2012), 11.

13. Ibid.

Chapter Four: Rafael Tello and the Faithful People of God

1. Enrique Ciro Bianchi, *Pobres en este Mundo*, 11 (see chap. 3, n. 13).

2. Ibid., 12.

3. Victor Manuel Fernández, commonly known as "Tucho" among his colleagues and students at the Catholic University of Argentina (UCA), was named rector of that institution by Cardinal Bergoglio. A few weeks after his election, as Bishop of Rome in 2013, Pope Francis made him a titular archbishop while remaining rector of the Catholic University of Argentina. In 2014, he was named vice president of the two sessions (extraordinary and ordinary) of the Synod of Bishops on Marriage and the Family held in Rome in 2014 and 2015.

4. Bianchi, *Pobres en este Mundo*, 39–40 (see chap. 3, n. 13).

5. Omar César Albado, "Volverse al Hombre Concreto: Una Aproximación a la Cultura Popular en la Teología del Padre Rafael Tello," *Vida Pastoral* 283 (2010).

6. This is the current author's English translation of text from Tello's unpublished 1988 manuscript titled *Fundamentos de una Nueva Evangelización*, n61, cited in Albado, "Volverse al Hombre Concreto," 2–4.

7. Juan Carlos Scannone, "Relación entre la Pastoral de Francisco y la Teología del Pueblo: Conversación con el P. Juan Carlos Scannone, SJ," *Vatican Radio*, April 2, 2014.

8. *Concluding Document of Aparecida*, nos. 262ff. (see intro., n. 3).

9. "Pope Francis: Address to CELAM Leadership," *Vatican Radio*, July 29, 2013.

10. Scannone elaborates on this and cites Pope Francis's meeting with CELAM bishops in Rio de Janeiro on July 28, 2013.

11. Thomas Aquinas, Commentary on John's Gospel, c. 6, lect. 3, n. 901. English translation accessed at http://dhspriory.org/thomas/John6.htm.

12. Tello cites St. Thomas Aquinas's *Summa theologiae*, I–II q.64 a.1, q.162 a.3 ad 1m. Tello develops these thoughts in more detail in *La Iglesia al Servicio del Pueblo*. Omar Albado explores the notion of the people's "knowledge by connaturality" in "Algunas características de la teología afectiva según el padre Rafael Tello," *Vida Pastoral* 288 (2010): 20–25.

13. Bianchi, *Pobres en este Mundo*, 218 (see chap. 3, n. 13), quotes from Tello's *La Iglesia al Servicio del Pueblo*, no. 30, and *El Cristianismo Popular según las Virtudes Teologales*, no. 34.

14. Jorge Mario Bergoglio, "Religiosidad Popular como Inculturación de la Fe," in *Testigos de Aparecida*, vol. 2 (Bogotá: CELAM, 2008), 281–325.

15. See Mark T. Miller, *The Quest for God and the Good Life: Bernard Lonergan's Theological Anthroplogy* (Washington, DC: Catholic University of America Press, 2013), 74–79.

16. Bianchi, *Pobres en este mundo*, 238 (see chap. 3, n. 13).

Chapter Five: Evangelization, Spirituality, and Justice

1. Cardinal Avery Dulles's posthumous study of evangelization is one of the more concise but thorough treatments of the subject in English. See Avery Dulles, *Evangelization for the Third Millennium* (Mahwah, NJ: Paulist Press, 2009).

2. Marcello Azevedo, *Vivir la Fe en un Mundo Plural* (Estella, Navarra: Editorial Verbo Divino, 1993).

3. Massimo Faggioli, "The Church and the World: Augustinians and Thomists," in *Vatican II: The Battle for Meaning*, 66–91 (see intro., n. 2).

4. Pope Benedict XVI, "Address to the Roman Curia Offering Them His Christmas Greetings," December 22, 2005.

5. Ibid.

6. Azevedo, *Vivir la Fe en un Mundo Plural*, 39–41.

7. See "Declaration on Religious Liberty," in *Vatican Council II: Constitutions, Decrees, Declarations*, ed. Austin Flannery (New York: Costello Publishing, 1996), 551–68.

8. Rachel Donadio, "Pope Addresses Secularism in France," *New York Times*, September 13, 2008, http://nytimes.com/2008/09/13/world/europe/13pope.html.

9. For a treatment of how Catholicism and science have related in a complementary way, see George Coyne and Agustín Udías, "Spiritual Foundations for Jesuit Commitment to Science," *Conversations* 47 (Spring 2015): 5–7.

10. Pope Benedict XVI, "Address to Courtyard of the Gentiles," *Origins* (April 7, 2011): 697–99.

11. See "La Misa Tango del Cardenal Bergoglio," *El Arca*, November 12, 2013, reported in the Argentine blog *Amor de la Verdad*, http://moimunanblog.wordpress.com/2013, or the *Rorate Caeli* blog at http://rorate-caeli.blogspot.com.

12. Azevedo, *Vivir la Fe en un Mundo Plural*, 43.

13. Christian Smith and Melinda Denton, *Soul Searching: The Religious and Spiritual Lives of American Teenagers* (Oxford: Oxford University Press, 2005).

14. John W. O'Malley, "One Priesthood: Two Traditions," in *A Concert of Charisms: Ordained Ministry in Religious Life*, ed. Paul K. Hennessy (New York: Paulist Press, 1997), 17.

15. Edward T. Hall, *Beyond Cultures* (New York: Anchor Books, 1976).

16. Azevedo, *Vivir la Fe en un Mundo Plural*, 43–44. Author's translation from the Spanish.

17. Ibid., 45.

18. *Catechism of the Catholic Church*, Second Edition (Rome: Libreria Editrice Vaticana, 1997).

19. "Preliminary Question Applicable to All Sections of the *Relatio Synodi*," Questions 41–43.

20. Azevedo, *Vivir la Fe en un Mundo Plural*, 48–49.

21. Ibid., 107.

22. *Document of Puebla*, no. 932.

23. See also Edward Yarnold, *The Awe-Inspiring Rites of Initiation: The Origins of the RCIA* (Collegeville, MN: Liturgical Press, 1994); and James Schellman, "Mystagogy—the Weakest Period of the Initiation Process?" *Catechumenate* (September 2010): 2–8.

24. Marcello de Carvalho Azevedo, *Oração na Vida: Desafio e Dom* (São Paulo: Edicões Loyola, 1988), 231. Author's translation from the Portuguese.

Chapter Six: An Emerging Pastoral Vision

1. *Concluding Document of Aparecida*, no. 19 (see intro., n. 3).

2. See Timothy Matovina, *Latino Catholicism: Transformation in America's Largest Church* (Princeton, NJ: Princeton University Press, 2012), 93–96; also Michael Connors, *Inculturated Pastoral Planning: The U.S. Experience* (Rome: Editrice Pontificia Universita Gregoriana, 2001).

3. Joe Holland, "Introduction: Roots of the Pastoral Circle in Personal Experiences and Catholic Social Traditions," *The Pastoral Circle Revisited*, ed. Frans Wijsen, Peter Henriot, and Rodrigo Mejía (Maryknoll, New York: Orbis Books, 2005), 1–14.

4. Pope Francis, "Informe a la V Conferencia del CELAM," in *Familia et Vita: Las Enseñanzas de Jorge Mario Bergoglio Papa Francisco sobre la Familia y la Vida 1999–2013* (Rome: Pontifical Council for the Family, 2013), 137–46.

5. Ibid., 143.

6. Ibid., 141.

7. George W. Traub, *Do You Speak Ignatian?* (Cincinnati: Xavier University, 2012), 12–13.

8. Benjamín Bravo, ed., *¿Cómo Hacer Pastoral Urbana?* (Mexico, DF: Ediciones Paulinas, 2013).

9. Sefania Felasca, "What Would I Have Said at the Consistory? An Interview with Cardinal Jorge Mario Bergoglio," *30 Giorni*, November 2007, http://www.30giorni.it/articoli_id_16457_13.htm.

10. J. A. Coriden, T. J. Green, and D. E. Heintschel, *The Code of Canon Law: A Text and Commentary* (New York: Paulist Press, 1985), 418–19.

11. Vatican Radio, November 27, 2014, http://en.radiovaticana.va/news/2014/11/27/pope. Author's emphasis.

12. John L. Allen, Jr. interviews Cardinal Francis George, "What 'America's Ratzinger' would like to ask Pope Francis," *Crux*, November 16, 2014.

13. Carlos María Galli, "Ternura, Alegría, Conversión, Misión y Reforma: La Teología Pastoral de Francisco en *Evangelii Gaudium*," unpublished conference at the Catholic University of Argentina, Theology Faculty, May 6, 2014.

14. Michael L. Budde, *The Two Churches: Catholicism and Capitalism in the World System* (Durham, North Carolina: Duke University Press, 1992).

15. See Carlos María Galli, "Diez Claves de la Exhortación *Evangelii gaudium* en el Contexto del Pontificado Reformador y Misionero de Francisco" (unpublished paper, Buenos Aires: Faculty of Theology, Universidad Católica de Argentina, 2014).

16. Cardinal Jorge Mario Bergoglio, "What I Would Have Said at the Consistory," interview by Sefania Falasca, *30 Giorni* 11 (2007), http://www.30giorni.it/articoli_id_16457_13.htm. Author's emphasis.

17. Pope Francis, "Informe a la V Conferencia del CELAM," 137.

18. *Concluding Document of Aparecida*, 44 (see intro., n. 3).

19. Cardinal Oscar Rodríguez Maradiaga, "The Importance of the New Evangelization," *Origins* 43, no. 24 (November 14, 2013): 374–75. Author's emphasis.

20. "Pope Francis: Address of Pope Francis to Members of the 'Corallo' Association," Vatican Radio, March 22, 2014.

21. "Pope Meets with International Theological Commission," Vatican City, December 5, 2014, http://www.zenit.org/en/articles/pope-meets-with-international.

22. Virgina R. Azcuy, "Evangelización con Espíritu," unpublished conference at the Catholic University of Argentina, May 6, 2014.

23. Cardinal Carlo María Martini quoted in a final interview before his death said, "The Church is 200 years out of date; the Church must admit its mistakes and begin a radical change, starting from the popes and the bishops," *Reuters*, September 1, 2012.

Chapter Seven: Implications

1. David N. Power, *Mission, Ministry, Order: Reading the Tradition in the Present Context* (New York: Continuum, 2008).

2. John T. Noonan, Jr., *A Church That Can and Cannot Change: The Development of Catholic Moral Teaching* (Notre Dame, IN: John W. Kluge Center Book/University of Notre Dame Press, 2005).

3. Martini, *Reuters*, September 1, 2012 (see chap. 6, n. 23).

4. Maradiaga, "The Importance of the New Evangelization," 374 (see chap. 6, n. 19).

5. Ibid.

6. See Junno Arocho Esteves, "Pope Stresses Importance of Widespread Presence of Women in the Church," *Zenit.org* (Vatican City), February 9, 2015, http://www.zenit.org/en/articles/pope-stresses-importance -of-widespread-presence-of-women-in-the-church.

7. See Benjamin Soloway, "Brazilian bishop urges ordination of married community elders as priest shortage grows," *Religious News Service*, November, 24, 2014.

8. See Antonio Spadaro, "A Big Heart Open to God," Interview with Pope Francis, *America*, September 30, 2013.

9. See Bill McGarvey, "Pope: Warns That Poorly Trained Priests Can Become Little Monsters," *America*, January 4, 2014, http://americamagazine .org/content/all-things/pope-warns.

10. The work of Sister Katarina Schuth, OSF, has been especially notable. See Katarina Schuth, *Seminaries, Theologates and the Future of Church Ministry* (Collegeville, Minnesota: Liturgical Press, 1999), 207–15.

11. USCCB, *Building Intercultural Competence for Ministers* (Washington, DC: USCCB Publications, 2012).

12. James Empereur and Eduardo Fernández, *La Vida Sacra: Contemporary Hispanic Sacramental Theology* (New York: Rowman & Littlefield Publishers, Inc., 2006).

13. Peter C. Phan, ed., *Directory on Popular Piety and the Liturgy: Principles and Guidelines* (Collegeville, MN: Liturgical Press, 2005).

14. O'Malley, "One Priesthood: Two Traditions," 16 (see chap. 5, n. 14).

15. Ibid.

16. Maria Teresa Pontara Pederiva, "A Social Market Economy Needs to Be Established, Says Archbishop Marx," *La Stampa*, January 26, 2015, http://vaticaninsider.lastampa.it/en/world-news/detail.

17. Andrea Tornielli and Giacomo Galeazzi, "To Care for the Poor Is Not Communism, It Is the Gospel!" *La Stampa–Vatican Insider*, January 11, 2015.

18. Pope Francis, "A good Catholic meddles in politics," *La Stampa–Vatican Insider*, February 28, 2015.

Conclusion

1. David Tracy, *The Achievement of Bernard Lonergan* (New York: Herder and Herder, 1970), 23.

2. St. Thomas Aquinas, *Summa Theologiae*, vol. 3 (New York: McGraw-Hill, 1964), 14. See also Marshall McLuhan, *Understanding Media: The Extensions of Man* (Cambridge, Massachusetts: MIT Press, 1964).

3. Gerard O'Connell, "Pope Francis' Spiritual Reform," *America*, February 16, 2015.

BIBLIOGRAPHY

Ecclesial Documents

Catechism of the Catholic Church, Second Edition.

Concluding Document of Aparecida. V General Conference of the Bishops of Latin America and the Caribbean.

Dives in misericordia (Rich in Mercy). Encyclical. St. John Paul II.

Document of Medellín. II General Conference of the Bishops of Latin America.

Document of Puebla. III General Conference of the Bishops of Latin America.

Ecclesia in America. Post-Synodal Exhortation. St. John Paul II.

Evangelii gaudium (The Joy of the Gospel). Apostolic Exhortation. Pope Francis.

Evangelii nuntiandi (On Evangelization in the Modern World). Apostolic Exhortation. Pope Paul VI.

Gaudium et spes (Pastoral Constitution on the Church in the Modern World). Second Vatican Council.

Lumen gentium (Dogmatic Constitution on the Church). Second Vatican Council.

Pastores dabo vobis (Post-Synodal Exhortation on the Formation of Priests in the Circumstances of the Present). St. John Paul II.

Quadragesimo anno (Encyclical on Reconstruction of the Social Order). Pope Pius XI.

Redemptoris hominis (The Redeemer of Man). Encyclical. St. John Paul II.

Rerum novarum (Encyclical on Capital and Labor). Pope Leo XIII.

Sacrosanctum concilium (Constitution on the Sacred Liturgy). Second Vatican Council.

141

General Bibliography

Albado, Omar César. "Volverse al Hombre Concreto: Una Aproximación a la Cultura Popular en la Teología del Padre Rafael Tello." *Vida Pastoral*, no. 283 (2010).

Aquinas, Thomas. *Summa Theologiae*. Vol. 3. New York: McGraw-Hill, 1964.

Aschenbrenner, George. "Consciousness Examen." *Review for Religious*, no. 31 (1972): 14–21.

Azcuy, Virginia, Carlos María Galli, and M. González. *Escritos Teológicos-Pastorales de Lucio Gera*. Buenos Aires: Libros Agape, 2006.

Azevedo, Marcello de Carvalho. *Vivir la Fe en un Mundo Plural*. Estella, Navarra: Editorial Verbo Divino, 1993.

———. *Oração na Vida: Desafio e Dom*. São Paulo: Edições Loyola, 1988.

Bergoglio, Jorge Mario. "Religiosidad Popular como Inculturación de la Fe." Vol. 2 of *Testigos de Aparecida*, 281–325. Bogotá: CELAM, 2008.

Bianchi, Enrique Ciro. *Pobres en Este Mundo, Ricos en la Fe*. Buenos Aires: Libros Agape, 2012.

Bravo, Benjamin, ed. *¿Cómo Hacer Pastoral Urbana?* Mexico, DF: Ediciones Paulinas, 2013.

Budde, Michael L. *The Two Churches: Catholicism and Capitalism in the World System*. Durham, NC: Duke University Press, 1992.

Catechism of the Catholic Church. 2nd ed. Rome: Libreria Editrice Vaticana, 1997.

Conners, Michael. *Inculturated Pastoral Planning: The U.S. Experience*. Rome: Editrice Pontificia Universita Gregoriana, 2001.

Coriden, Joseph A., Thomas J. Green, Donald E. Heintschel. *The Code of Canon Law: A Text and Commentary*. New York: Paulist Press, 1985.

Cortés Conde, Roberto. *The Political Economy of Argentina in the Twentieth Century*. New York: Cambridge University Press, 2009.

Dulles, Avery. *Evangelization for the Third Millennium*. Mahwah, NJ: Paulist Press, 2009.

Faggioli, Massimo. *Vatican II: The Battle for Meaning*. New York: Paulist Press, 2012.

Fernández, Eduardo, James Empereur. *La Vida Sacra: Contemporary Hispanic Sacramental Theology*. New York: Rowman and Littlefield, 2006.

Finding God in All Things: A Marquette Prayer Book. Milwaukee: Marquette University Press, 2009.

Flannery, Austin, ed. *Vatican Council II: Constitutions, Decrees, Declarations*. New York: Costello Publishing, 1996.

García Hernán, Enrique. *Ignacio de Loyola*. Caracas: Taurus, 2013.

Hall, Edward T. *Beyond Cultures*. New York: Anchor Books, 1976.

Hennessy, Paul K. *Ordained Ministry in Religious Life*. Mahwah, NJ: Paulist Press, 1997.

International Theological Commission, *Sensus Fidei in the Life of the Church*. Rome: Libreria Editrice Vaticana, 2014.

Ivereigh, Austen. *The Great Reformer: Francis and the Making of a Radical Pope*. New York: Henry Holt and Company, 2014.

Lonsdale, David. "Ignatian Spirituality." In *The New Westminster Dictionary of Christian Spirituality*, edited by Phillip Sheldrake. Louisville, KY: Westminster John Knox Press, 2005.

———. *Listening to the Music of the Spirit, the Art of Discernment*. Notre Dame: Ave Maria Press, 1993.

Maradiaga, Oscar Rodríguez. "The Importance of the New Evangelization." *Origins* 43, no. 24 (November 14, 2013).

Matovina, Timothy. *Latino Catholicism: Transformation in America's Largest Church*. Princeton: Princeton University Press, 2012.

McDonagh, Francis. *Dom Helder Camara: Essential Writings*. Maryknoll, NY: Orbis Books, 2009.

McLuhan, Marshall. *Understanding Media: The Extensions of Man*. Cambridge, Massachusetts: MIT Press, 1964.

Miller, Mark T. *The Quest for God and the Good Life: Bernard Lonergan's Theological Anthropology*. Washington, DC: The Catholic University of America Press, 2013.

Noonan, John T. *A Church That Can and Cannot Change: The Development of Catholic Moral Teaching*. Notre Dame: University of Notre Dame Press, 2005.

O'Malley, John W. *The Jesuits: A History from Ignatius to the Present*. New York: Rowman and Littlefield, 2014.